SKY LANTERN

*The Story of a Father's Love for
His Children and the Healing Power of
the Smallest Act of Kindness*

MATT MIKALATOS

HOWARD BOOKS
AN IMPRINT OF SIMON & SCHUSTER, INC.

NEW YORK   NASHVILLE   LONDON   TORONTO   SYDNEY   NEW DELHI

Howard Books
An Imprint of Simon & Schuster, Inc.
1230 Avenue of the Americas
New York, NY 10020

First Howard Books hardcover edition November 2015

HOWARD and colophon are trademarks of Simon & Schuster, Inc.

For information about special discounts for bulk purchases, please contact Simon &
Schuster Special Sales at 1-866-506-1949 or business@simonandschuster.com.

The author is represented by Ambassador Literary Agency, Nashville, TN.

Manufactured in the United States of America

10   9   8   7   6   5   4   3   2   1

Library of Congress Cataloging-in-Publication Data

   Mikalatos, Matt.
     Sky lantern : the story of a father's love for his children and the healing power of
the smallest act of kindness / Matt Mikalatos. — First Howard Books hardcover edition.
       pages   cm
     "Howard Books non fiction original hardcover" —Title page verso.
   1. Mikalatos, Matt. 2. Mikalatos, Matt—Correspondence. 3. Mikalatos,
Matt—Blogs. 4. Mikalatos, Matt—Family. 5. Father and child. 6. Fathers
and daughters. 7. Paper lanterns. 8. Fathers—Death. 9. Kindness. 10. Mental
healing I. Title.
   HQ755.85.M535   2015
   306.874'2—dc23

                                    2015026477

ISBN 978-1-5011-2349-8
ISBN 978-1-5011-2350-4 (ebook)

Contents

CONTENTS

1

Picking Up

Broken things gather in my front yard.

On Wednesdays the garbage truck lumbers through our neighborhood in Vancouver, Washington, squeezing between parked cars. By Saturday the missed bits of trash, blown by the wind, assemble on the last street of our neighborhood. Empty aluminum cans, scraps of pizza boxes, plastic forks, and crushed water bottles get caught in rose thorns or shoved into the grass, half clinging to the sidewalk, arranging themselves in a semicircle in front of my house.

Our houses pile up close to one another in suburban con-
formity. A plum tree stands guard at every corner. My house
stands at the western edge of our cluster. A fence runs alongside the street. When my wife, Krista, and I first moved here,
we had no money for landscaping, so I scoured the Internet
for free plants. I drove twenty miles to collect what looked
like a pile of dead branches. Dropping the brown, thorny
canes into the narrow strip of dirt yielded a thriving forest of
Old World roses called Chapeau de Napoléon. Every spring,
heavy pink blooms appear. They don't last long, but they're
intensely fragrant. It's amazing what a small bit of water, sun,
and dirt can do.

I occasionally peel the jungle of roses away from the fence
to clean out the trash wedged into the briars. Discolored
aluminum cans with energy drink logos crowd alongside
microwave burrito wrappers and yellowed single sheets from
newspapers. Once I found an entire unopened can of cat
food, a tiny gray and white tabby face staring at me from deep
in the forest of thorns.

It's a maddening ritual, picking up the trash that skitters
across our front lawn. So you can imagine why I thought the
sky lantern was nothing more than a larger-than-usual piece
of refuse at the end of my driveway.

The driveway isn't long—about the length of a car. From

the front window of my house I could see what appeared to be a large, clear bag plastered half on the sidewalk, half on the driveway. I sighed when I saw it. It was a Saturday, and it had rained hard the night before, and I didn't want to trudge the twenty-five feet from my front door to the sidewalk to peel up someone else's trash, then hike it back to the garbage can.

Saturdays are rarely days of rest in our house in any case. Our fourteen-year-old daughter, Zoey, has tennis, and twelve-year-old Allie has ballet. Myca, our five-year-old, enjoys the constant shuttling and preparations, and will happily tag along in the car, watching the world through the rain-streaked windows. Like any household with five people, there is cleaning and bickering, the making of food and the grudging cleanup, the tinny sounds of screens singing in the background and the shouts when someone can't find something and the time to leave has arrived.

Picking up is a large part of our lives. It's a rare day not to find a lone sock on the couch. Never the same sock, of course, which is to be expected, because my kids don't wear matching socks. Matching socks is a quaint obsession of their elders. I pile wayward belongings at the bottom of the stairs, hoping the kids will carry them up to their rooms. Allie piles backpacks and ballet bags in the entryway to the house, which she insists on calling "the closet" even though it's a roughly two-foot-square space that must be navigated by every person in the house.

By the time Saturday comes, I'm tired of picking things up. My things, other people's things, picking up the kids at their activities, from school, picking up the mail or the dry cleaning or the pace or whatever else has fallen and needs to be lifted again. So, I admit it, I didn't want to pick up the trash at the end of the driveway and hoped that Krista might do it.

But when Krista bustled Zoey into the car, both of them dangling tennis rackets, and backed into the street, driving over the deflated bag, I knew it would most likely be one of my chores for the day. I knew my wife had seen it, because she called me an hour later and said, "There's a bag or something at the end of our driveway. I ran over it this morning."

I was halfway through getting Myca's shoes on, her pitifully mismatched socks staring at me while she sang a song and kicked and laughed and Allie, upstairs, shouted, "I can't find the bobby pins!" I wedged the phone between my shoulder and ear, knowing the right response and finally bringing myself to say it.

"I'll pick it up," I said. Later. Because right now I needed to get Allie out the door and on her way.

We swirled into the car, Allie and Myca singing a nonsense song together as we navigated northward and dropped Allie off for her day's worth of dance. Myca and I pulled back into the driveway thirty minutes later. Krista and Zoey were home now. She had driven over the bag again, of course. I saw the tire marks as I pulled alongside it.

It had begun to rain again. Nothing like the previous night, which had been a rare storm of window-rattling fury, but it was wet nonetheless, and Myca ran to the porch, shouting and leaping before bursting into the house. I went to the porch, too, my hand on the doorknob, debating whether to pick up the trash and be done with it.

I did not want to pick up the garbage. It was such a little thing, but in my mind it had taken on unreasonable proportions. It wasn't my trash. I didn't throw it there. Why had it rained last night? If it had been dry, no doubt the bag would have scuttled to the end of the cul-de-sac, and one of my neighbors would be debating who should pick it up.

I sighed and walked down the drive, the rain plastering my hair to my scalp. I bent down and discovered it wasn't plastic. It wasn't a bag. It was translucent paper attached to a bent wire frame. This was not what I had expected, and all my cranky reluctance disappeared, replaced with mild curiosity.

I peeled the paper up from the sidewalk. A short note in

Sharpie was scrawled on one corner: "Love you, Dad. Miss you so much. Steph." The stark, unexpected statement of love startled me. How did this come here, to my house? There was another line of text, a short and innocuous bit of writing that didn't hold my attention. But those two sentences, followed by a hastily scribbled heart and her name—I couldn't stop staring at them.

I lifted the paper completely from the ground. It wasn't a bag at all: it was a sky lantern. Burnt-out and crumpled. Broken. Sky lanterns are like hot-air balloons, only much smaller. This one was made of paper and metal. The candle was long gone.

Something about that note filled me with a sudden melancholy. Maybe it was the rain. The thought of this young woman—was she young? I didn't know that for sure—sending a note to her father, through the rain, which landed here, at my house, made the world seem hollow and sad for a moment.

I set the lantern down and smoothed out the paper, my hand running across Steph's words. I slipped my phone out and took a picture of her note. I wanted to remember it; I wanted to think about it.

That morning I had begrudged the journey from my house to the driveway and back. Now I wondered if the road ahead of me was much, much longer. I wondered where this note might take me.

Where had the lantern come from? Could I retrace its journey? Would that be a good thing? It must be from someone nearby. I shivered because of the cold, not because I was thinking of some fatherless girl out there—a daughter missing her father.

I put the lantern in the recycling. Before I made it into the house, I stopped and pulled up the photo on my phone. I wanted to see the note again. I stood in the driveway, halfway between the trash can and the front door, looking at the picture on my phone. The rain dripped down my face, into my eyes. The photo blurred, covered in drops of rainwater.

I wanted to find Steph.

I wanted to tell her I had found her lantern.

I wanted to tell her it was going to be okay.

For once, I told myself, for once I wouldn't throw away the broken things that gathered here. For once I was going to fix it. Somehow I was going to fix it.

But was that even possible?

Probably not.

This woman, Steph, she might not even want to hear from me, may not want to know where the lantern landed. Not that I had a single clue to go on, anyway. It was foolish to think there was anything to be done other than to throw the lantern away and go about my day.

I put the phone in my pocket and put the lantern out of my mind.

There was nothing I could do.

2

A Light in the Darkness

THE FIRST TIME I SAW A SKY LANTERN, I WAS IN KRABI, Thailand. It was 2008.

Krista and I had a work conference in another part of the country the week before. Several hundred American interns from all over Asia had come together for a week to decompress and get training, and my wife and I were two of the coaches. I was also one of the main speakers for the week. I would pull myself together every morning, take deep breaths, walk across the expanse of green lawn behind our hotel, and steel myself so that I could speak without my voice shaking . . . so that I could get through forty minutes of teaching without crying.

Jet lag can fray your emotions, and leaving Zoey and Allie with my parents for a week added to the sensitivity, but by far the hardest thing was that Krista had been pregnant the day before we left.

She called me while I was out running errands, Zoey and Allie both strapped into their car seats. I don't remember exactly what I was buying. I think maybe chocolate bars for Krista, maybe some granola bars for the plane. We were leaving in less than twelve hours.

I don't remember everything she said, but I do remember two words: "I'm bleeding."

I called my mom and asked if I could drop the girls at her place, and she said yes, even though I hadn't told her what was going on. I sped back to the house, and Krista and I barreled to the hospital like an ambulance with no lights or siren, cars moving out of our way because of our desperate speed and reckless impatience.

Too late.

Krista was in her thin hospital gown, crying. I was beside her, also crying. Was it supposed to hurt this much?

The ultrasound showed nothing at all. An empty, perfectly healthy womb. The miscarriage had probably taken place a while ago. There was nothing we could have done; it wasn't our fault, it was just a thing that happened.

The nurses let us sit in the emergency room for a while, Krista flipping listlessly through TV channels, waiting for the drugs they gave her to kick in. She hadn't been pregnant long. These things happen, the doctor said. One in three, she said, and she was right: this was our third child.

We were mourning, but not because we knew this child. We were mourning her possibility. We had rearranged our lives getting ready for her, making a space for her in our house, in our routines, in our family. We had told Zoey and Allie, and they were so excited. We had told our parents. Now she was gone and there was nothing to be done.

Six hours before departure, we debated whether we should get on the plane. We decided to go. It would be good to see our friends, to keep busy, to be with the interns, to have the colorful sights and pungent tropical smells of Thailand to keep our minds from the half-converted office space that was her bedroom, and from the nearly unpacked boxes of Allie's hand-me-down baby clothes.

So I stood every morning in the wonder of Thailand, explaining to a room of interns how to thrive overseas while I was struggling to thrive myself. Still, the warm air and pool, our friends, and the space to think and process was welcome.

Our parents brought the kids to meet us at the end of the week. We'd been planning this family vacation for some time. Our parents get along well and sometimes vacation together with us. They are brave, generous parents to take their grandchildren on an international flight, and we were happy to see them. We met our two bouncing balls of energy and two sets of grandparents after the conference and set out for a house Krista's mom had found for us all to share.

The house was great. Our packed white van dropped down a narrow path from the highway through thick trees to a set of properties alongside a bay. Our house was built in a U shape around a swimming pool, with three bedrooms clustered in independent villas, all facing the pool. Krista and I took a room. My parents, Pete and Maggie, took the kids in theirs, and Krista's parents, Janet and Terry, took the third.

In the mornings, Zoey and Allie would wake up far too early from the jet lag wanting to swim. A few Thai women arrived with the sun and made an enormous breakfast. The whole family gathered at a wooden table on the pool deck and ate pancakes, fresh pineapple, bananas, bacon, toast, and eggs. We watched the slow rise of the sun over the bay. I would lie in the hammock as the day warmed, and the kids returned to swimming. We read books, took the days slow, wandered on long walks, played cards, fed the koi in the pond behind the house, took a bus into town to watch a movie.

It was exactly what we needed.

We laughed every day. On one of our walks, we went through a nearby Muslim village. Zoey, seven years old at the time, was walking beside me. All of our kids have gone through Spanish immersion at their school, and it has given them a unique love of other cultures and a great view of the world. This particular day the villagers had slaughtered a cow, and the head was hanging in a tree as we walked by. Far from being disturbed by the grisly sight, Zoey seemed enormously fascinated.

"What is that?" she asked.

"What do you think it is?" I wanted her to tell me her own observations.

She said, "Looks like someone is getting ready for a fiesta!"

She thought the cow's head was a piñata. That brought a smile to my face the rest of the day despite the lingering sadness of the miscarriage. The fresh way that kids look at the world brings healing in a way little else can.

In the afternoons the bay outside our house emptied, leaving behind a vast mudflat. At dusk the water came in again, and Thai fishermen pulled their boats up through the shallows, lugging their catch to shore. As the sun set, we would gather as a family again and eat a traditional Thai meal. Allie, five years old, made us laugh because she was the only one who could stomach the spicy shrimp. She popped them into her mouth one after another, the rest of us crying from the spice, she with a grin on her face as she pulled the serving dish close to her own plate.

When night came, I tucked the girls into their narrow beds in my parents' room. We talked about the day, and I sang to them and told them stories and prayed for them before they slept. They sank into glassy-eyed almost-sleep, worn-out by the day and jet lag. I waited for them to drift off, my own limbs heavy from grief more than fatigue.

All was quiet. Krista and our parents were playing a game of dice, laughing at the table. I wandered outside past the pool, away from the light of our house, across the long yard that led to the bay. A wooden chair sat facing the water. From that chair I could see lights bobbing in the black distance, and could just make out the shapes of small islands. The stars were bright and insistent, but I felt the blanket of darkness more acutely than the pinpricks of light. A chorus of night insects trilled their evening song, the pitch rising and falling. A fish jumped in the bay, the small splash sending concentric circles of water racing for the edges, the expanding wave visible by the glint of starlight on black waters.

There was life here—and moments of joy—but they were like the stars: rare burning spots in a lifeless void. I didn't feel numb but thought numbness might be a welcome relief. The loss of our child stabbed in every quiet moment. She had a name, and now we had no need to speak it. She had a future, or so we thought, and now nothing. We had made a place for her in our future, but her only place now was in our shared history. The universe was made up of darkness, and any light was both distant and insufficient.

Someone shouted from the yard next to ours, a cry somewhere between alarm and delight. I couldn't see them— couldn't see much of anything in the darkness—but I turned in their direction.

A jellyfish descending from the sky. That was my first thought. A gently glowing, flickering, warm-hearted sky lantern dropped toward me, the slight breeze moving it toward the bay as it slid through the warm night air. I could see the neighbors now in its warm glow, jumping from their chairs, shouting, running after it as it coasted across their yard. And then I jumped from my chair, too, and found myself taking tentative steps toward it.

It glided to the ground, its paper shell bending as it skidded through the grass, then regained its shape. One of the neighbor's teens ran after it, grasped it, and danced with it over her head. Her hair shone in the lantern's light, and her brother ran behind her, both of them giddy with laughter.

Then the brief flame flickered out, but I could still see them, just barely. I could still hear them as they laughed and twirled and danced through the dark. I could hear the paper lantern crinkling beneath their fingers and imagined a life in which children ran through the grass unaware of the darkness around them.

I had been startled out of grief by wonder.

I closed my eyes and could see the afterimage of that warm light tracking across the sky.

3

What I Knew

I couldn't stop thinking about Steph, whoever she was.

I had made the assumption that her dad was dead. But it was possible, wasn't it, that her parents were divorced? Or that he was serving overseas and she hadn't seen him in a while? Who knew, in the end, why she had sent that lantern?

I figured she must live nearby. Most sky lanterns have small fuel cells, essentially treated cardboard or a small candle, and fly for ten or fifteen minutes. Plus, there had been a brutal storm the night before, with winds heavy enough to knock over my barbecue grill in the backyard. Tree limbs had fallen. The storm had rattled the windows and apparently forced the lantern down in my yard.

There's a park half a mile to our west. I wondered if she could have launched it from there. Or maybe from the trailer park across the highway. Or any of the neighborhoods clustered against our own. Who knew? Maybe it came from farther than that. I live in Vancouver, Washington, right on the border of Portland, Oregon. Maybe it came from Portland somewhere. Or even Seattle. I guessed that might be possible.

I made a mental checklist of what I knew, and it wasn't much.

There was a person named Steph. Presumably female. Looking at the handwriting, I didn't have much doubt about that.

She missed her dad. Again, the most likely guess was that he was gone. Dead. Otherwise, wouldn't she just send him an e-mail? A text? Pick up the phone? No, it seemed likely he had passed away. How to communicate with the dead—that was a difficult question. Writing on a sky lantern seemed like a reasonable attempt.

I knew when it had landed in my yard: November twenty-second, the Saturday before Thanksgiving.

That was it. No address. No phone number. No last name.

It was almost time to pick up Allie from ballet. Myca was standing by the bookshelves I had built with her grandpa Terry, playing with little plastic animals. She whispers while she plays, so I can't always tell what the animals are saying. I love when I can understand the words, though. Myca is quite a character, and even though she's only five, she has strong feelings on a lot of topics.

For instance, she's a born vegetarian.

She has eaten almost no meat in her entire life, despite the fact that we have meat at least one meal a day in our house. She refuses, and has since she started solid food. She would spit out baby food with meat in it. We would wrap tiny bits of beef in rolled-up spheres of white bread and she would suck on the bread and spit out the beef.

Hot dogs, hamburgers, chicken, fish, it doesn't matter. She won't eat it. Once, when she was about three, I was playing with her toy animals with her. I was the lion, and she was a giraffe. I had the lion attack a lamb, and Myca walked the giraffe over and said, "Hey, that's not nice. Lions shouldn't eat other animals." Speaking for the lion, I asked what he should eat, and Myca said, "These berries and leaves are nice for a lion to eat."

Myca will eat one type of meat, and I'm sorry to say it's partly based on a deception on my part. She will occasionally eat a chicken strip. She won't eat chicken "nuggets," but if it's a "strip" made from real chicken breast, she'll sometimes eat one. When she was little and asked what it was, I told her it was "bok bok"—you know, the sound a chicken makes. So she ate bok bok for a while.

The weird thing was that she would only eat them frozen: she'd gnaw on them cold. Krista and I debated whether this was good for her, but finally figured they were fully cooked and we should let the poor girl get some protein.

Meanwhile, it was time to put shoes on and make our way through the rain to pick up Allie. Myca doesn't like to walk to the car when it rains. Sometimes I make her walk, but she likes when I sling her into my arms and run—which, as near as I can tell, gets us both wetter than walking. Today we ran.

Myca doesn't require much entertainment in the car, and never has. She likes to watch the world pass by. She has the best sense of direction of anyone in the family, and has been able to direct a car back to our house from most places in town since she was three years old. She's probably a genius. A weird vegetarian genius.

With my daughter quiet in the backseat, I had more time to think as we drove.

What if Steph didn't want a response? Or, rather, what if she didn't want a response from me? If she was trying to communicate with her dad, it was entirely likely that she didn't expect a stranger to find the note and send a letter back. If she did, wouldn't she have included a way to contact her?

I could think of only one possible way of writing her back: posting a letter on my website, which could feel like an invasion of privacy to her. Maybe she wouldn't want her personal information out there. Maybe she wouldn't want me talking about her relationship to her dad in front of a bunch of strangers.

On the other hand, would she ever see it? If she never saw my response, it wouldn't matter what Steph's intention was or whether it was an invasion of privacy. But if she never saw it, why would I write it in the first place?

Allie got into the car, her face flushed from ballet. I drove toward home, and she and Myca started singing along to a Taylor Swift song. They were dancing, laughing, acting like maniacs.

I thought about Steph's dad. I wondered what he would want.

I tried to put myself in his position. What if I had died and my daughters wanted a connection with me? What if they sent out a sky lantern that said "I love you, Dad" and it landed in the yard of some other, living father? What would I want him to do? Throw it away and forget about it?

No way. I would want him to find my kids and tell them one thing: your dad loved each of you.

Whether they sent the lantern looking for hope or a moment of private healing or on a whim or because they were asking for help, I would want them to know I loved them. I would expect any good father who found that lantern to tell my kids that. Because there has to be some sort of fraternity of fathers, doesn't there? Some agreement that if one of us is unable to care for our kids, then the rest will pitch in?

As we pulled into our neighborhood, I thought about Zoey and Allie and Myca and tried to imagine what it would be like for them if I died. I knew they would still have their mom and two sets of grandparents and aunts and uncles who loved them and would be there for them. That's not even counting all our family friends. But that would have been true for me, too, as a kid, and I couldn't imagine how painful losing my dad would have been. I knew Steph, wherever she was, no matter how supportive the rest of her family, must be in a lot of pain.

Thinking about my own kids trying to connect with me after I was gone, wishing they had a dad, got me all choked up. Thinking about not seeing their faces every day made the road ahead blurry.

I knew Steph's dad must have felt the same way. I knew that whatever Steph wanted, her dad would want me to reach out, to try to make a connection.

I pulled into the driveway. I had made my decision. I would write Steph a letter. She would probably never see it, but maybe my kids would. Maybe someday they would be at my funeral and someone would remember, "Oh, hey, your dad wrote a letter once about how fathers feel about their kids. I think it's on his website," and maybe they would read it and maybe for a few minutes they would feel my love for them, sitting in the house after the funeral, wearing their black dresses and huddled together around a computer.

Or maybe nothing would come of it. But I knew I had to try.

4

The First Sky Lantern

OUR FAMILY LIVED IN CHINA FOR THREE YEARS. ZOEY WAS three months old when we first arrived there, and she was a source of pride, love, and wonder for the entire city. People would crowd around us on the street to see her. There weren't many foreigners in this particular town, and even fewer with children, so Zoey was well-known in our neighborhood. Although she had dark hair and eyes (a source of infinite confusion for many of our Chinese neighbors, who wanted to know if she had a Chinese grandparent), her skin was white, which brought many comments about how she looked like a porcelain doll.

One day I timed how long it took for Zoey to draw a crowd. In less than a minute, sixty people gathered around her stroller, all with their hands behind their backs, leaning over, straining to see her. In China, there is a series of questions adults ask about infants to show their interest in the child: "Is she cold? Does she need another blanket? Are those socks warm enough?"

This only increased when our next daughter, Allie, was born. Zoey has thick, gorgeous dark hair and deep-brown eyes, showing off her Greek heritage. When the nurse first picked up Allie she said, "Oh! A redhead!" I didn't believe it until she was washed and handed back to me. She has beautiful red hair.

As most redheads will tell you, strangers often use a child's red hair as an excuse to be patently rude. It baffles me that a complete stranger would comment about a child's paternity. It can be aggravating, but Krista has a great way of keeping things in perspective. She often helps me to get over things and focus on what matters. So when I say, "People are thoughtless idiots sometimes," she will respond with something like "Let's be gracious anyway."

So, more than once, Krista and I found ourselves explaining to complete strangers about red hair being a recessive trait, meaning you must have the trait in the family history on both sides, and, no, neither parent needs to have red hair for their children to have red hair.

My favorite story about this is when Allie was three or four years old and we were at a restaurant for a nice family meal, when the waitress asked her, "Where did that red hair come from?" and Allie said, "From God." Then my daughter, deadly serious and with great patience and kindness, added, "Your hair comes from God, too."

Our three children are as distinct and wonderful as the seasons. Zoey, our April baby, dark and beautiful and arriving with the early spring flowers. Allie, cool and gorgeous as winter. Myca, like a beam of summer sunshine, light and full of music.

We loved living in China, the four of us. In fact, the older two girls occasionally look at Myca and say, "I wish you had lived in China." They feel sorry that she was born in the US and never got to experience living abroad. The people in China are friendly and they love kids in a way that's different than in the United States. When we went to restaurants, the servers would pick up the kids and carry them off to see the fish in their aquariums, or into the kitchen to watch the chefs shaking the woks and chopping the broccoli. When we went on walks, people would offer the kids food or ask to hold them. Zoey's first solid food came from an old woman on the street who held out a whole shrimp on chopsticks. Zoey ate the whole thing, legs and all, to the considerable delight of the woman and her friends.

There were difficulties, too, of course, like the fact that Zoey was allergic to Chinese diapers. They caused a rash wherever they touched her. And the fact that Zoey's favorite Chinese baby food flavor was "fish and carrots," which gave her breath like a cat. But, looking back, one of the things we loved about being in China as a family was that help was always hovering nearby. The whole community was simply waiting to be asked to step in. Every man in town was "uncle" and every woman was "auntie." Say the word and they would step in to take care of your child, because every child is precious and the whole city is their family.

This played out in a hundred different ways, whether it was people offering to hold Zoey and Allie when we went shopping, or the kind elderly couple who ran a convenience store downstairs from our apartment who would come running out whenever they saw us to load us down with free cookies, or lollipops, or milk, or seaweed crackers. (Both Zoey and Allie loved seaweed crackers.) We were reminded daily of how close help was. One day a woman ran across traffic, weaving between giant blue trucks and tiny honking commuter cars before crossing a stream of bicycles to hand me a pair of socks from her purse. Zoey had kicked hers off, and the woman had noticed from across the street. Help was always nearby.

Which brings us back to sky lanterns. Sky lanterns are a call for help, too. Or at least that's how they started. We're told they were invented by a man named Zhuge Liang, called Kongming, in a town not far from where we lived in China.

The story goes that Kongming and his people were trapped in a town called Pingyang. Kongming was one of the greatest military minds of his time, and was a renowned inventor and diplomat as well. He was also connected to the literary community. He was a man with many talents. But his great nemesis, Sima Yi, had cornered him in Pingyang. Kongming couldn't get a message out to his allies. He was trapped, with no help to be found.

Until he came up with the idea of a sky lantern. Using bamboo to make a lightweight skeleton and oiled rice paper to cover it, he took a small candle and set it underneath to make the lantern fly. He took brush and ink and wrote a note on the paper of the lantern, explaining the situation and asking for help. He made many such lanterns. Then he ascended the city wall and studied the winds.

When the wind was blowing in the right direction, Kong-ming lit the candles and released the lanterns, which flew high over his enemies, descending into the eager hands of his allies. It wasn't long before he knew the message was received, for he saw the dust of a great army headed toward Pingyang. His message on the sky lantern had been received, and help was on the way.

It had been a day and a half now since I found the sky lantern. It was Sunday night. Myca was in bed, and I could hear Krista and the older kids moving around downstairs. I needed to be alone to respond to the sky lantern note. I often write in the same room with the family while everyone is watching television or talking about their days, but tonight I needed the quiet.

I knelt down next to my bed, using it as a table. It's not a posture I usually take, but it felt somehow reverent that night. I pulled open my laptop and started to write. I told Steph how I had found her lantern and how I had debated writing back to her. I told her a little about my own kids and why finding the lantern meant something to me.

Then I wrote a letter with everything I'd want to say to

my daughters if I couldn't share with them anymore. About a third of the way through I had to stop and take a break. I took deep, shuddering breaths and considered what I'd written so far. I felt good about it. I worked to finish it, polishing it as I went along. All told, it took me about an hour and a half to write. I wanted to get the letter out into the world as soon as possible, but thought I would wait for morning. I scheduled it to post early Monday morning.

I didn't mention it to Krista or my kids. In that moment, it felt like something private. I knew it wouldn't stay that way. I knew it would be public come morning, and some of my friends and family would read it. I knew my kids would come across it someday, years from that moment.

I didn't expect what was coming. I had no idea how far the letter would travel in a few hours, or how many people would see it and share it and pass it along to others.

That night I closed my eyes in the darkness of my bedroom and slept while the words of the letter flew through the dark spaces between my computer and the next, moving fast and far, much farther than the sky lantern itself had flown.

When morning came, everything had changed.

5

The Letter

Here's the letter I wrote to Steph:

An Open Letter to Steph, Who Sent a Sky Lantern to Her Father, Which Landed in My Driveway

Dear Steph,

Saturday morning I noticed what I thought was a gigantic plastic bag plastered to the end of my driveway. I didn't think much of it at first, other than to say to myself, well, there's another piece of trash that has found its way to my yard, I guess I'll be the one who has to pick it up.

Which I did not do. Not at first.

So it sat there in the rain for a while.

In the afternoon the rain slacked off, and during one of my treks from the front door to the car, headed off to shuttle my daughters to their various activities, I saw it again. I thought again about how it had become one more chore on my to-do list.

When I came closer I saw that it wasn't plastic at all, it was thin, wax-coated paper, tangled with a bit of twisted wire. You had written on it, which is how I know your name and why you sent that lantern off in the first place.

You wrote "Love you, Dad. Miss you so much" and then a heart, almost but not quite careless, and then your name.

I thought about this a lot during the day. I thought about you, and your dad, and how something happened, and you're not together now. I assumed that your father has passed away. I thought about this as I picked up my middle daughter from ballet. As I took my eldest to youth group. As I tucked my youngest into bed for the night.

I debated whether you'd want to know where your sky lantern ended up. I wondered if you had sent the lantern up, sending a message to your dad and hoping for one back, and if you would prefer to believe that it went up, up, and never came back down. I wondered if you preferred to think it had found a place in a constellation rather than torn and flattened on my driveway.

Then I wondered if maybe, somehow, your lantern landing in my front yard was a sort of answer from your dad, because I'm a dad, too. And your message stuck in my heart. I know a day is coming when my three girls won't have an easy way to get ahold of me. They won't be able to crawl in my lap while I'm reading, or send me a text, or shout for me from upstairs. They won't be able to call or send me an e-mail. I can imagine they, too, might send a sky lantern. Or leave me some flowers and talk to a shiny square stone with my name on it.

I thought about my kids, writing a note to me on a sky lantern and sending it off. I knew immediately that if it was my kids, and their sky lantern, I would want the father who found that lantern to tell my kids a few things.

So, here it goes, Steph. If I were your dad, here's what I would want to say to you. Here's what I'd want to say to my own daughters:

I have always loved you.

From the first moment I held you I knew there wouldn't be a deeper love in my life. There's this fierce protectiveness that settled in, and I knew I would give anything to keep you safe, to provide you a good life. We had our moments. We fought sometimes. I did stupid things. I made mistakes, and so did you. But no matter what happened, I loved you with a deep, unalterable, unending love that surprised me, because I had never felt anything like this, ever. I know I told you I loved you . . . more than once. But in retrospect it wasn't often enough, could never be often enough to express the depth of my love. There were these moments, sometimes, when I watched you and you didn't know. You'd be sitting on the couch, or doing the dishes, or working on homework, or singing some ridiculous song with your friends, and I'd have this sudden rush of affection for you. But I let you keep going. I didn't want to interrupt you. I wish I had taken one more moment to say it one more time. I know you know this, but I will say it again: I love you. So much. Don't ever doubt it. Past, present, future. Always.

I am immensely proud of you.

Kids wonder if their parents are proud of them. I know, that's natural. Maybe it's because I love you so much, but

I've always been proud of you. I was so pleased when you said your first word. When you stood up. When you walked. Now look at you. Writing sentences on sky lanterns! Okay, I know writing a sentence is not terribly impressive, but you have to understand that you've grown from this tiny bundle who couldn't speak or move or do much of anything other than cry and sleep and now you're this fully formed human being who makes decisions and works and speaks and alters the world as you move through it. That's an incredible thing. You've made mistakes and kept going. You've shown love to people around you, sometimes complete strangers. You make the world a better place. You do! Believe me, I've bragged about you to plenty of people whether you saw it or not. You're one of the greatest accomplishments of my life. Better than any painting by any famous artist. More important than anything any politician has done. You're unique, you're amazing, and you're my daughter. Of course I'm proud!

Live a good life.

If you can make yourself a better person, do it. If you can change the world for the better, or your family, or your neighborhood, or your state or country, then go take care of it. The good life doesn't always mean the easy life, so don't be afraid to sacrifice and work hard to build a life that brings you joy. Remember that selfishness rarely pays off the way you think it should. Don't let work consume you. Make space for family and friends. Laugh. I hope you laugh a lot. I know that's hard sometimes, and I know life is hard. I know you miss people. I know you miss me. I'm not saying those relationships can be replaced, but find new ones. Find kindred spirits to run through life with you. Eat meals with them. Go see crappy movies and make fun of them. Go watch your friend's kindergartner play soccer in the rain. Pick adventure over entertainment. Do something meaningful and amazing. Be happy. Build a habit of thankfulness, and a life full of things to be thankful for.

Be loved.

There are these relationships we find ourselves in that drain us constantly. You know the ones I mean. The people who always have a reason why you should do things their way. The ones who imply you're a bad person because you have your own opinion. The manipulators. The guilt-makers. Don't waste your life on them. Find people who understand how precious you are, and who aren't afraid to tell you so. Find people who will say hard things to you because they want you to grow and have a better life, not because they're trying to control you. Be brave. There are people out there who will love you. You deserve that. Go find them. Don't let them go. Fill your life with them.

I know your dad would want someone to say those things to you, Steph. "I have always loved you. I am immensely proud of you. Live a good life and be loved. You're an incredible woman." I know he would want to tell you that he wishes he could be with you, that he's sorry you miss him, and that if he could change things to be with you, that he would. He would want you to live a full, beloved, beautiful life. I hope you are.

And, Steph, one more thing.

The fact that you love your dad so much is a sure sign of how much he loved you. He's not here now, but accept the love that comes from the people around you. Let them be his sky lantern back to you. Let them share their love, and let that be a reminder of his. No one will ever love you quite the way your father did, but many people will see in you some of the same qualities and beautiful bits that he did.

Love is as strong as death. As inevitable, as powerful, as eternal. It can't be escaped. It can't be avoided. It won't be forgotten.

And when death is gone, love will remain.

Sincerely,

Matt

6

"Edelweiss"

OUR MONDAY MORNING RITUAL LOOKS LIKE THIS:

At seven a.m. we roll out of bed. Myca gets a bowl of cereal. She tells me what color bowl she wants in Spanish (usually *amarillo* or *rojo*), and I set it out for her and pour the milk. Zoey wanders into the kitchen and makes some oatmeal. Allie doesn't have to get up until later, so she'll often get in bed with Krista and talk for a while before breakfast.

Meanwhile, I make Myca's lunch, a peanut butter and

jelly sandwich and some crackers. We have now exhausted nearly all the things Myca eats. Eventually, Allie descends and makes her breakfast. Krista cooks her oatmeal on the stove. I don't usually eat breakfast, but some mornings I'll make myself half a peanut butter sandwich while making Myca's lunch.

Everyone scatters to get themselves ready. Our daughters go to three different schools, so we have a semicomplicated drop-off schedule. I walk Myca to kindergarten, about five blocks from our house, and then come home to drive Zoey to middle school. When I get back, either Krista or I drive Allie to her school, an arts school downtown.

Myca likes to ride her scooter to school. It's a Razor scooter, pink with purple streamers shooting off the handlebars. Myca has been riding scooters since she first learned to stand. She used to have a red three-wheeled Radio Flyer that she rode in the house. We spent years with her zooming from the living room to the kitchen to get a glass of water and back again. She would cry if we tried to put it in the garage.

So she races to the school on her scooter and I half jog to keep up with her, carrying her pink Hello Kitty backpack over one shoulder or, if it's raining, running along with her tiny pink umbrella over my head, like I'm some sort of exotic tropical drink. We say good morning to the various neighbors we see along the way, like Gary, who is often walking his white mop-furred dog, Bobo.

When Myca was two, "bobo" is what she called rainbows. She loved rainbows. She would stand at the living room window whenever we saw one through the backyard, staring at the colored arc for ten minutes at a time, saying "Bobo, bobo" over and over. She would often cry when they faded away. Bobo the dog always confused her. She thought he was named after rainbows. Bobo was the first dog Myca would pet regularly, no doubt because of his name.

We pass the crossing guard. Despite the fact that almost everyone is driving by the school this time of morning to drop off their own children, they are maniacs about getting through the intersection. A good crossing guard steps into the danger zone with confidence, giving the impression that she will crush any cars that dare to keep moving forward. We say good morning and give the guard our thanks.

As I walk Myca toward the school, I take her scooter and lug it over one shoulder, then take her left hand with my right. I usually pray for her as we walk—a short, simple prayer that I prayed every day I dropped my older girls off at school, too. "Dear God, give Myca a good day. Teach her a lot about You and this world You made."

When I drop her off in the gym where the kindergarteners line up, she invariably forgets that I still have her backpack.

"Did you forget something?" I ask her.

She peels herself away from her friends and comes trotting back to me, a sheepish smile on her face. Every morning that same sheepish smile. Then she says, "Oh, yeah, my backpack."

I get down on one knee and sling it off my shoulder, getting it situated on her back. She acts like she's going to leave, then turns back, grins at me, and gives me a hug and a kiss. I tell her I love her, and she says she loves me, too. Then she runs to her friends, not turning to look back or watch me leave.

I know this won't last forever. My older girls still want to get hugs and kisses, of course, and still say that they love me every day. They're not embarrassed to say it in front of their friends, or if they are, they've never let me know. This walk to school, rain or shine, the small things like holding hands as we approach the school—those things are only going to be ours for a few more years.

It's strange how these things pass. There are times when it seems like they'll never end, like you're going to be in this pattern forever. For instance, getting Zoey and Allie ready for bed when they were kids used to be a big, involved affair.

There were rituals. I told stories or read books. They shared a room, so there were rules about whose bed I sat on and when. The stories would sometimes be made-up, sometimes from books, sometimes repeats of previous nights.

But every night, one ritual was the same.

Every night, I would sing "Edelweiss" to them. I don't re-member how it started, except that it's a slow, beautiful song. I used to sing different songs, and one night I sang that one and then it was all that would be allowed.

It's a haunting, beautiful song, originally written by Rod-gers and Hammerstein for the 1959 musical *The Sound of Music*. I first heard it in the movie version. My kids hadn't seen the movie, but they loved the song. In the musical, the patriarch of the Von Trapp family, Captain von Trapp, sings the song as an act of patriotism for his country in the face of the Nazi occupation, as well as a way of saying good-bye to his beloved homeland. It's a song about loss and beauty, and how in the midst of change there is hope that things might stay the same. Whatever may come, edelweiss still grows in the mead-ows of Austria.

To Zoey and Allie, it was a lovely song about a beautiful white flower that would last forever, and they liked that the flower would greet them every morning after they slept. I have stood in the dark doorway of their bedroom a thousand times, singing that song to them. When they were small, just the first few bars of the song would make their eyes droop. As they got older, they would sing it together with me from their beds, their thin, high voices floating together with mine.

Somehow, one of my friends at work caught wind of this family tradition, and at a company picnic in the mountains of Colorado, she told an entire region of our company about my nighttime ritual. My family was there with me, so the girls came up in front of the crowd, each of them holding one of my hands, and we sang "Edelweiss" together. Me, the kids, my coworkers and their families, all of us singing about tiny Austrian flowers.

Things change. I haven't sung that song to Zoey and Allie in years. Myca hates it! She would rather have what we called "the mockingbird song" ("Hush, Little Baby") or maybe "Sing, Sweet Nightingale." In fact, she much prefers Krista singing. So, for Myca, Krista has done the lion's share of the singing, mostly "Hush, Little Baby." Myca did go through a brief phase in which she wanted me to sing "Love You Like a Love Song" by Selena Gomez as a lullaby, which is more difficult than you would think. I suspect she thought it funny to see me crouched by her bed, trying to turn a pop song into a sweet lullaby.

So the time to sing "Edelweiss" has passed. It was a sweet tradition when it lasted, a way that I told my kids I loved them without ever saying the words. I would call and sing it on the phone when I traveled. Krista told me I should record it so they could hear it whenever I was away.

Now the older girls get a good-night and quick kiss and they're off to put themselves in bed—no story, no singing. Myca gets two books and I pray for her, give her a kiss, and turn out the lights.

We have new ways to communicate. Things change, they shift, they move on. I used to get so sick of singing "Edelweiss." I sang it every single night for several years, and it wasn't always enjoyable. Sometimes the kids would fight over where I should stand, or if they should sing along or just listen. Then one night we didn't do it for some reason. Maybe a few nights in a row. Then we sang it once a week. Or once a month. Then somehow I realized I hadn't sung the song in half a year. A year. It had just passed on, out of our lives. It wasn't a thing we did anymore.

On the morning I posted the letter to Steph, our ritual changed. I was downstairs, getting Myca breakfast. While I was leaning against the sink, enjoying my half of a peanut butter sandwich, Allie came into the kitchen in her checkered flannel pajama pants, a tousled T-shirt on, her hair hanging in her face. She wrapped her arms around me and gave me a long hug.

"I read your letter," she said, and then went back upstairs.

I went upstairs to my room to find Krista crying. "Allie came in and asked me if I had seen your letter," she said.

It was my first indication that the letter was doing something more than I had expected. I pulled up my website. The letter had more than thirty comments already. People started sharing it on their social media. It was spreading, mostly to people I knew. Friends and acquaintances.

I was glad it had already provided a reminder to one of my daughters that I love her. It was a new way to connect, a new way to say it. That's part of growing up with your kids: finding the new way to tell them they are loved, to say it in a way that they believe you. It's not always easy, making that shift. But I was glad she knew.

I wish I had known the last night I sang "Edelweiss." I wish someone had told me, "This is the last time you'll sing good-night to your kids in this way, the last night it will mean what it does to them right now." Maybe I would have stretched out the notes a little longer. Or maybe I would have repeated it more than once. Maybe I would have stood there in the dark by their beds and listened to their breathing slow as they sank into peaceful sleep.

But we never know those things. We never know if this time we say "I love you" will be our last, or the last time we will say it in quite that way. In the next few days I would hear from people all over the world, telling me their stories of their own fathers, of fathers who loved them but couldn't quite say it, or who loved them and had passed away and had been unable to say it for many years. Or, for some, fathers who never showed any sign of love, or even showed evidence of the opposite.

I couldn't have known any of those things, either. Who knows how far a simple love letter will travel? Who knows how far a sky lantern, with a simple phrase of love scrawled on the side, will fly? None of us have any idea.

So we have to keep singing it, keep saying it, keep writing it, keep showing it.

We have to send our love out into the world so others will find it.

7

Notes from Strangers

THE LETTER HAD BEEN UP LESS THAN TEN HOURS BEFORE I was overwhelmed by notes from strangers. Comments on my website, on various social media platforms, and a few e-mails, too. Most of them came from people who had lost their own fathers. It started with friends of friends and moved out from there, in widening circles, as more and more people sent it to their loved ones, to those who had experienced loss, with fathers sending it to their children and mothers saving it to show to their own children when they grew up.

It was gut-wrenching to read some of these stories. One woman wrote to tell me her husband had died a few months before, leaving her and their three small children behind. She would be saving the letter to show them when they were older, she said. A woman wrote to tell me that her father had died when she was young, and she had printed the letter out and folded it in her purse. It made her feel closer to him.

I figured the least I could do was write back to each person, telling them I was sorry for their loss and wishing them peace, healing, and joy in the year to come. I cleared my schedule to answer the notes. Many wanted to know if I had found Steph, but there hadn't been any sign of her. A few people had written, wondering if it might be a family member of theirs. I answered each one, but so far no one had written back to say, "Yes, I think it actually is my sister." I hadn't expected to find Steph anyway, but then again I hadn't expected a response like this, either. On the first day, my website had tens of thousands of visits.

I also started getting notes from various websites and media outlets that wanted to share the story. The first was a site for men, trying to show that men are more complex than the alpha male representation portrayed in some media.

They liked the tender side of the letter and wanted to post it. I told them they could, of course. A site for moms also wanted to run it, as did a site in Latin America that wanted to translate it into Spanish. I had to send that request to my friend Amanda, because, as near as I could tell, it was a site that sold placenta pills or something, and my Spanish is restaurant Spanish. *Mas burritos, por favor* is about as complicated as I get. Amanda assured me my terrible Spanish was the problem, not the website.

I never expected this kind of interest. I shared my letter on the regular social media websites I post to and my blog, but it's not like I was intentionally advertising it. The response was shocking.

One week had passed since I found the note. I remember, because it was trash day again, the day before Thanksgiving, and we packed up to go to my in-laws' house. We spend most holidays together with both families. Krista's parents and mine and whatever siblings and other extended family are nearby will all pile into one house or another and celebrate together. Our friend Shasta often joins us, because she's part of the family, but this year she was headed to Montana to be with her folks. This year we were spending Thanksgiving at Krista's parents Terry and Janet's house, so we packed a few days' worth of clothes into the car, along with the children, and started our drive south to Corvallis, an hour and a half away.

When all five of us squeeze into one car for a trip, there are predictable results. At some point a war breaks out about the music on the radio. The kids start jockeying for position in the back, their elbows sharpened to points. Allie likes to spread her feet out, and because she's extremely flexible, you might discover a leg draped over your shoulder as you drive. Zoey is as territorial as an alligator. Myca is five, which means she can't be reasoned with. And, of course, Krista and I are normal adults, prone to bouts of claustrophobia, terrors, and psychosis in such tight quarters. Nonetheless, we did fine. Krista had wisely packed snacks and drinks, and the kids were tired, which meant more disagreements on the front end but naps in the near future.

We hadn't anticipated the traffic. Or, rather, we hadn't anticipated the traffic being quite so bad. We knew it wouldn't be great the day before Thanksgiving, but we didn't expect it to be a parking lot all the way from Portland to Corvallis.

I was driving. My phone started buzzing, and since we were moving at three miles an hour, I felt safe stealing a glance at the caller ID. It was my friend Wes Yoder. It was strange that he would call just before a holiday, especially because we had exchanged e-mails that morning, and he had told me he was packing up for his own Thanksgiving travels.

I had written him that morning, just a quick note telling him about the letter. I thought he'd want to know. He had written back to say he was on his way out for the holiday but would get back to me later, and then written again to say, "Oh my gosh, I'm crying now. This isn't even fair to make me cry like this . . . but, oh, so beautiful."

Wes is an amazing guy. I met him because he's a literary agent (in fact, he's now my agent!) and we quickly became friends. He's the sort of guy who collects interesting people and introduced me to a few fascinating characters. He's also kind, wise, and calm. He walks into a room and makes everyone feel more at peace. I call him sometimes just to listen to the things he'll say.

Having said that, he and I don't usually talk on holidays, because we both have plenty of family. So I knew he was calling about something important. I handed Krista the phone and she put it on speaker for me.

"Hi, Wes! Happy Thanksgiving!"

"Happy Thanksgiving, brother." Wes always calls me brother. "Have you found Steph yet?"

"Not yet." We talked about the letter for a bit, but I could tell Wes had something bigger to talk about.

"This morning when you sent me the letter, I forwarded it to a few people." This wasn't a big surprise anymore, as it seemed like everyone was doing the same. "Some of my friends at the *Today* show reached out and asked if they can publish it on their website."

"What?" It wasn't that I hadn't heard him; it was that I needed to hear it again to believe it. So he said it again. The *Today* show wanted to run it on their website and wanted to make it available to their various news affiliates and *their* websites, but they needed permission from me. Wes walked me through the sort of note they needed. They wanted it right away, too, which was a bit of a problem, since I was sitting on a highway packed with cars, with no end in sight. If I found Steph, they wanted to know right away.

"Do you still have the lantern?" Wes asked.

Umm. Well. It was in my recycling, sitting out on the curb at my house. Even if we could turn around and get home, we'd already made more than an hour's headway going south. The recycling truck had likely come to get it already. It was gone. All that remained was the one picture I had taken of it. "It's gone," I said. "I had no idea it was going to be a big deal. I guess I should have saved it."

We never know what little act will be important later in our lives. For me, at that moment, it was picking up a piece of trash a few days earlier. I hadn't wanted to do it, and now look what had happened. Looking back, I wish I had held on to the sky lantern or at least cut out the piece with writing on it. I could have dried it out and framed it. I could have kept it as a souvenir or kept it in case I met Steph one day.

But now the *Today* show wanted to share the letter. Maybe Steph would see it. Certainly they had a larger reach than me. I pulled off the highway and into a Burgerville parking lot. While the kids used the restroom and bought more snacks, I sat behind the steering wheel typing out a permission letter with my thumbs.

The letter would go live the next morning, Thanksgiving Day. I felt thankful already. I hoped more people would read the letter and find some hope this holiday season. And maybe that it would find its way back to Steph.

8

Thanksgiving

THANKSGIVING MORNING! KRISTA AND HER PARENTS WERE already cooking when I woke up. Some years, Krista grows her own pumpkins in our backyard. She babysits them, she waters them daily, and she happily reports on their size as they fill out and take over the garden. Then, come Thanksgiving, she makes fresh pumpkin pie. Terry, my father-in-law, was stuffing the turkey. Krista and her mom, Janet, were getting an apple tart ready for the oven.

The television was on so we could watch the parade in New York City. Growing up, it seemed like the parade was supposed to be a bigger deal than it actually was. My parents wanted us to be thrilled to see Spider-Man (and I guess I was, a little). My kids barely spared it a glance. For my parents growing up, this parade was a moment to see all their favorite cartoon characters come to life. For me, even as a kid, that wasn't so special. I could look to my lunch box or action figures to see them. As for my kids, they can see their favorite characters on demand. Of course, the ultimate moment of the parade is Santa Claus arriving on his sleigh—a moment that once heralded the beginning of the Christmas season. I'm pretty sure that season now arrives on November first. As soon as Halloween has ceased making money for the stores, it's time to roll in Christmas.

So the television was on in the background as the family swirled into action. Krista and her folks toiled away in the kitchen. My parents were on the way with appetizers and side dishes. Krista's brother Kevin and sister-in-law Shimmra were headed over with my nephew Jonas, and Aunt Diane and Grandma Traylor were on their way. Four generations of family, all packed into Janet and Terry's lovely home in the woods, toasty warm with an oven that had been baking since early that morning and would continue all the way through until turkey time.

The kids were on vacation, which meant they couldn't be easily separated from their blankets or electronic devices. The promise of cookies, pie, and snacks eventually got them up and moving.

I don't get much cell reception in Terry and Janet's house, so I brought out my laptop. There was an e-mail from Wes with a link to the *Today* show website. I pulled it up and there was my name. I was a "Today.com contributor." They'd posted my letter. The comments had already started. The *Today* show had also made the article available to all their NBC affiliates, so some news stations had posted it on their websites. Now there was no way I could keep up with all the comments, as much as I wanted to. I would stumble on a dozen new iterations of the post on various sites, all of them with comments. Some sites had thirty or more comments by the time I found them.

We needed two tables for the family to eat together. There was a lot of standing up and stepping over to the other table to deliver or receive dishes of steaming hot Thanksgiving food. I love Thanksgiving. More than other holidays, it seems like the focal point is gathering with loved ones and spending time together, even if that time is largely spent cooking, eating, cleaning up, and sleeping it off.

My mom used to try to jump-start little traditions for

Thanksgiving when I was growing up. For a few years we would invite people without family to come join us, even though we barely knew them. I didn't mind that at all, actually. It was fun to have new faces with us for the holiday. The other tradition I remember clearly was my mom handing out kernels of unpopped popcorn: we would take turns putting the kernels in the middle of the table, sharing one thing we were thankful for each kernel. We'd go around the table, talking about the good things in our lives.

It's a nice holiday. I like having a day when we talk about the things we're grateful for, and I couldn't help but imagine that must be hard for those who were reading my letter and remembering their missing loved ones. It's hard to sit around that Thanksgiving dinner table and see an empty chair. But in the comments online, I saw evidence of thankfulness. People were reminded of the love their fathers had for them, and they were deeply thankful for that. They were thankful for their good memories. They were thankful for the time they had together, and thankful to be reminded of their fathers.

It's a good practice, trying to turn our attention toward thankfulness. When my family lived in China, it was sometimes hard to remember to be thankful on Thanksgiving. We were inclined to really miss friends and family back home. There was no parade on television. We couldn't buy turkey, or cranberry sauce, or stuffing, or any number of traditional American foods in the local stores.

But we made it happen, and there were many reasons to be thankful along the way. Krista and I went to a local hotel and asked them if we could buy one of the imported turkeys they used in the restaurant, and they said yes. Then the head chef came out and talked to us for a while, and when we went to pick up the turkey—we had been told it would cost over a hundred dollars!—the chef had left instructions to give it to us as a gift.

Some American friends from our language class agreed to host the big meal, and we all worked hard to make it seem like home. Someone bought sweet potatoes, and someone else found a way to make stuffing. We couldn't fit the turkey in the short oven, which was only about twenty inches tall, so we cut the turkey in half with a buzz saw, right down the middle, and cooked it in two shifts.

One of my most vivid Thanksgiving memories comes from that day in China riding my bike in a sea of bicycles, half a turkey in the basket on my handlebars, the other half in a plastic bag hanging to the side. For everyone else on the road it was just another day, but for me and my family it was a day full of gratitude. Krista had everyone write letters about things they were thankful for on cream paper, and she glued them around thick candles. We sat at a long table in the glow of the candlelight, covered in thankfulness, surrounded by close friends and our best interpretations of traditional Thanksgiving foods, and I found, merely by stopping to think about it, that I had many reasons for which to be thankful—even far away from home, in a country that doesn't celebrate the holiday.

It's too easy to lose sight of this. I noticed in my own family a while back that the five of us moved toward a place where we were focused on the difficult things—the places where life didn't precisely line up with our expectations. We had become a family who spent a lot of time complaining. This happens sometimes, and it wasn't something to be ashamed of, but I wanted to see if we could change that.

We tried to start a new family tradition. Each night when we sat down to dinner, we would go around the table and everyone would share three things they were thankful for. Three things a day, no matter how terrible your day. It was okay to say, "I'm thankful school is over," or "I'm thankful tomorrow will be a new day."

Honestly, there were days when it was hard to come up with three things, especially when we first started. We had to add a couple of extra rules. For instance, no repeating what others shared. We can all be grateful for eating pizza, but we can think of a few more things to give thanks for, too. We actually put a one-food-item-per-family-member rule in place. When backed into a corner, my family is pretty thankful for food.

Here's the thing: if you can't think of three things to be grateful for, even on a pretty terrible day, something is wrong. I'm sitting in a hospital typing these words while our family friend Shasta is in the operating room. The doctors are checking to see if her breast cancer has spread to her lungs. It's terrible. This is not a good day. I'm not happy, and neither is she or our other friends who are waiting for the news. But I'm thankful she's my friend. Thankful for competent doctors. Thankful we live now and not a hundred years ago, and that medical knowledge has advanced.

That's what I explained to my kids. You can always give thanks. Everyone on earth should be thankful for oxygen. Being able to take a deep breath. Being able to sit at the dinner table with family. Having enough money to buy the food. Living in a green and beautiful corner of the world. We tend to compare ourselves to those "better off" than we are, which leads to bitterness and dissatisfaction, instead of appreciating where we are and what we have.

A couple years ago I spoke at a conference in Beirut, Lebanon. It was a grueling trip, about twenty hours from my house in the Portland, Oregon, area to the home of my host. Usually on these long trips I have a layover in Frankfurt, Germany, and there are these wonderful airline lounges where I can take a shower and get a snack. There are even beds where I can lie down for a few minutes and grab a nap. But on this particular trip there was a misunderstanding, and I found myself sitting sideways on a hard plastic chair outside the lounge, eating an airport pretzel. Granted, the mustard was excellent, but it didn't make up for all I was missing in the lounge. I landed in Beirut exhausted and rehearsing a letter of complaint to the airline.

At the conference, I met a woman from Jordan. She and a group of people from her community had taken a bus to Lebanon to come hear me speak. She told me how they had worried about land mines. How they had to stop before the various checkpoints and figure out whether they were run by Muslims or Christians so they could put on the right type of clothing. For a few hours a sniper was shooting at them and blew out a couple of the windows. "But I am so thankful you have come to speak to us," she said. "I know it is a hardship for you to come so far, and to leave your family for the week. Thank you!"

I didn't know what to say. Suddenly I was grateful for my smooth trip, during which I could relax in a safe chair in an airport and enjoy a pretzel, while this woman had crouched on the floor of a bus, covering her head, hoping not to be hit by flying glass. I should be full of thanks.

And I was. As my family gathered together around the Thanksgiving meal that year, all of us warm and happy, laughing, passing around the great food, then clearing the table and making space for dessert, I was thankful. Thankful for my family and friends. Thankful for where I live, thankful that my parents and Krista's parents get along so well and that we don't have to choose between them at the holidays. Thankful for my kids. Thankful for my nephew's habit of making cookies the size of the baking sheet he bakes them on. Thankful to live so close to so many people I love.

I opened my e-mail again that afternoon and found something else to be thankful about: I had an e-mail from a stranger. My eyes scanned through the paragraphs. ". . . saw your letter . . . family passed it on to me . . . sky lantern . . ."

Then the last three words of the e-mail: "Thank you! Steph."

Steph had found me.

9

Circles

ONE OF THE MOST MEMORABLE LETTERS I RECEIVED AFTER the sky lantern post was from a woman named Anuradha Chandran Menon. For this note to stand out is impressive, because every day I received letters that made me weep. Krista asked me to stop opening my computer in bed each morning because sometimes she would read over my shoulder and we'd both be crying. "I can't start every morning this way," she said.

But Anu's letter, and the picture she sent me, are so beautiful and interesting and reflect the communications of many others who have written. This is the note she sent:

Blessed Matt,

I am writing from Malaysia. Saw this post on my niece's Facebook wall and somehow I knew I needed to read what you wrote. This is so weird but not unusual. Was suddenly very down today with thoughts of my father flooding in. Usually when this happens, my dad will find some means to console me . . . this time it's what you wrote to Steph.

I am a "Steph" too. Lost my beloved father on Jan 11th 2011, exactly 1 month after I got remarried. He had what was his 6th heart attack, but unlike all the other times that he managed to pull through for us, this time it was a "switch off." Devastating was hardly the word to describe what I felt at that moment. Then 251 days later on Aug 13th 2011, my darling mummy followed him too. She battled stage 4 Ovarian cancer for 7 years. The 3rd relapse took her.

All of this haunts my brother and me until today. But we have accepted this. With faith that they are closer than ever now. Just a heartbeat away I would say. And the best part, one fine beautiful day, they will be there with arms

wide open saying "Welcome Home." I haven't set free a
sky lantern yet . . . must do that one day. But I write my
feelings down . . . be it pen and paper. Or paint to set my
pain free.

So much I would love to say to you. But as for now, bless
you Matt for crossing my path and sharing this message. It
sounded so much like what my "Acha" (what I call my dad)
would say. Thank you for these good tears. Thank you for
restoring Faith. Thank you.

Attached is a painting, a mandala I did back in 2011 in
honour of my father. Found some sort of closure after that.

You can see a photo of Anu's mandala in the center of this book. It took her seven days to finish, and each day she reflected on a different aspect of her father and her feelings toward him as she painted.

At the center of her feelings about her father, there's a crescent of white moon, partially eclipsed, overlaying a bright yellow circle with questing rays that could be a flower or the sun. Ringing that floral star comes another layer, with muted colors and sharp geometric shapes on the interior curve. Then it bursts into petals, each one filled with its own feathered star. From there it shoots into carefully balanced leaves until at last the brightness intensifies into a series of purples, nearly blue, that compete with golden yellows, merging into a pattern not unlike peacock feathers as it moves, at last, to the edges of the canvas.

The word *mandala* comes from a Sanskrit word for *circle*. A mandala is a type of symbol used often in Hinduism and Buddhism, although other religions, including Christianity, use them or something similar. Depending on the religion or the branch of the religion, they can be used for different things: to focus one's attention, as a meditation aid, to create sacred space, or to represent the universe.

Really, almost everyone who uses a mandala is, in some way, using it as a microcosm: a tiny replica of the universe we inhabit. There is a center of some sort, and out of that center come concentric rings of life, color, and patterns, and at the outer edges, an end.

Endings. We're defined by them, in some sense. If you look at human artwork, you can't help but notice that all paintings have edges. All stories wind their way to "the end." Songs, even inordinately long songs, are over in a few breaths. That's the way we think: Beginning. Middle. End.

When the edges arrive for those we love—when their story ceases to intersect with our own in any way we can easily sense—we are, understandably, distraught. The mandala in some way brings order to this. The mandala Anu made took her seven days, and each day revealed something else about her feelings about her father.

Her father and his love created a certain gravity, and part of her life orbited his, drawn in by their shared history and their love for each other. When he died, her own life felt out of control. New patterns emerged. The orbit shifted. In the midst of that chaotic repositioning, she sought a way to re-establish the circles in order to bring stability and find peace.

It's no wonder that, when we lose a loved one, we keep circling back, trying to find them. Even when we know there's no way for them to come to us, we keep lifting our heads when the doorbell rings, thinking maybe it could be them. We keep track of the days. We put photographs in a special place of honor. We acknowledge the anniversaries of their birthdays as well as their deaths.

Anu sent me a series of poems she wrote about her father, all of which were beautiful and reflected these themes. In one of those poems, called "101 Days," she shared her feelings 101 days after her Acha's death. She wrote these words:

> *When my days are spent trying to numb myself . . .*
> *Yet in the silence of my nights . . .*
> *When I lay myself down to rest . . .*
> *When I no longer cover myself with office work . . .*

TV serials, and whatever other chatter . . .

In the silence of the night . . .

The tears are painful, endless and silent . . .

Eyes that miss seeing, ears that yearn to hear,

Arms that hopelessly seek to hold close . . .

a heart that longs to speak . . .

In the silence of the night . . .

all that happened 101 days back . . .

just floods back into my mind . . .

In our grief, we can't escape the absence of our loved ones. Perhaps this is partly because our patterns have been broken, but we keep returning to them regardless, circling into old behaviors. We pick up the phone to call on Dad's birthday. We expect him to show up at the golf tournament or join us for a favorite movie. We wait for him to help decorate for the holidays. And then we remember and we are crushed. The pattern has changed, but we have not.

So we move on. The easiest way to do that is to break the patterns. To set them aside, forget about them, build a new life without that person, without their gravity. But we will miss the old ways—we might even miss things that once drove us crazy. We try to comfort ourselves. We try to find peace in ignoring their absence. We try to find peace in numbness. Over and over, we keep coming back to those painful memories of being happy once. And with those memories is the realization that we can never be happy again, not like that, not in that precise way, not with our loved one gone.

For some of us, there comes a time when a symbolic action can take our angst and grief and provide some measure of healing. It's a reminder that we are still connected somehow to our loved ones. For Anu, it was writing poetry and painting. For Steph, it was writing a love note on a sky lantern. Anu said in her original note to me, "I am a 'Steph' too." I received many notes that started with those words.

"I am a Steph.

"I am someone who has lost my father. I am in need of his loving words. I want this letter to be my letter, I want those words to be for me. I am in pain. I miss him. I love him."

Then they would share their story and the story of their loved ones. How they passed. How long ago. How they felt in the aftermath. What they hoped for the future. It was beautiful. Every note was a sky lantern. Every letter was a mandala. All of them were communications sent out into the universe, meant in some sense for their loved ones, but also a call for help—a signal flare to say, "I have lost someone important to me and need a new pattern, a new way of living, a new orbit."

Steph's lantern and my letter to her was providing a place where people were reminded of the old pattern, the place in their lives that had orbited in relationship to their loved ones who were gone. They were being reminded that although their fathers had passed on, perhaps their love for their children remained, and that it was okay for those children's lives to intersect the spaces that had been their fathers'.

It was permission to accept love again.

It was a reminder to embrace life.

It was an encouragement to be at peace, to seek hope, to live.

So they told me, over and over, every day, the letters piling into my inbox.

To interact with all these Stephs was a great honor, but I still hoped to find the "actual" Steph—the original—the one whose lantern had somehow, inexplicably, landed in my front yard.

I was waiting for that letter that said "I am Steph" instead of "I am *a* Steph."

And at last, that letter had arrived.

10

"Steph"

MY OPEN LETTER SHARED WITH THE WORLD STEPH'S LOVE
note to her father, but I hadn't shared what else was written
on the sky lantern, which I hadn't even mentioned to my
wife. There was a short line of inconsequential text. I didn't
keep this a secret because I thought I was being smart or because I believed it was an important or personal line of text. I
didn't mention it because I didn't think it mattered.

On Thanksgiving Day, I heard from a woman named Steph.

She thought it might be her lantern I had found. She wasn't completely sure: she had written on the lantern several months before and didn't remember exactly what she had written. She also lived on the East Coast, in a place where the lantern would have had to fight the prevailing winds to somehow make it to me. I wrote her back and apologized for her loss and asked her if she remembered the other thing written on the lantern.

She never wrote back. I was disappointed. I assumed this meant she probably wasn't the same Steph who had sent the lantern I found.

The day after Thanksgiving, I got another letter from a second woman with a similar story. She had sent a lantern—maybe this one? Did I think it could have traveled from her to me?

Within a few weeks I had been contacted by a variety of Stephs, all of whom said they had sent the sky lantern. As of today, I've been contacted by about seven Stephs who have lost their fathers and written on lanterns. Plus one Sherri, who apparently hadn't read the note carefully and thought maybe she had sent it, which I thought was truly funny and sweet. Some of my friends wondered if these women were interested in attention, trying to scam me, or just confused, but I don't think it was any of those things.

I think these women saw a note from a father that they

desperately wanted to be theirs. They wanted it to belong to them. They wanted not just to be moved by a stranger's letter but for it to be their letter. One sweet woman actually copied the note from the sky lantern in her own handwriting to show me it was the same as hers.

I realized when reading the first note that my job couldn't be to decide who was Steph and who was not. How would I know? Who was I to tell some grieving daughter, "No, my open letter to Steph wasn't for you"? I didn't believe that. I didn't think my letter was for one person. Even as I wrote it, I was thinking of my own kids, not only Steph. So how could it be for just that one person, whoever she was, who sent the sky lantern?

Other people felt the same. Notes, comments, and e-mails started with, "I, too, am a Steph." But those same notes were signed Tammy, Nicole, Amy, and a hundred other names. Many people had read the letter and realized it was for them because they needed to hear those comforting words. They had lost their fathers, and they needed to be reminded that their fathers loved them, were proud of them, and wanted them to live good lives.

So I had different types of notes coming in: "I am Steph" or "I am a Steph" and sometimes "I know a Steph" or "I know the real Steph." Some people wanted me to reach out to their siblings or loved ones and write them a note saying that I knew they were the ones who had sent the lantern.

All of these urges and desires came down to one thing, I think: the desire for there to be meaningful communication from beyond the grave. The hope that, somehow, our loved ones are reaching out to us. Not just to "us" but to *me*.

It's not my place to say whether that happens or how it happens. I didn't want to be the caretaker of "You are Steph" or "You are not Steph." Disqualifying someone felt too close to saying, "Actually, this note is not for you," which felt too close to "Your dad didn't love you," which I neither believed nor wanted to say.

So I did my best not to make a judgment.

I sent a lantern years ago and have a vague memory that I wrote something to my father on it. Could this be mine? It could be, I said, and I'm so sorry for your loss.

I am writing from impossibly far away, and to get from me to you the lantern would have flown against the wind. Could that be my lantern? Of course it could be. I hope the letter will bring you some peace and a reminder of your father.

Could it by my sister's sky lantern? I don't know if she actually sent one, but her name is Steph and we lost our dad and what do you think? I think your father would want you to know that he loves you and your sister very much.

Meanwhile, the letter spread beyond the United States. First to English-speaking countries. Then someone translated it to Spanish, and someone else to Portuguese. I got letters from Malaysia, China, Germany, and countries in eastern Europe. Some people sent pictures of their fathers. I remember one vividly: a middle-aged man wearing a crumpled white dress shirt. It looked like he might have come straight from work. He was in the hospital, his arms wrapped around a newborn, and he was looking up at the camera. His eyes were half-shut, which at first I thought was because of the timing of the photo, but on further study I realized it was because he was looking down at his daughter. He couldn't bear to look away long enough to take a picture.

It took me several full days to respond to all the notes as they came in, and I know I missed some. A few got replies that sounded nearly identical to the last. But I tried, as much as I was able, to pause and think about each note and write something back that expressed the care, love, and concern that their own fathers would have felt for them.

On December sixth, I got another note on social media saying, "We found Steph!" I didn't think much of it, because I had heard it several times already. I had, at this point, heard from about eight Stephs. I had no doubt this most recent woman was someone named Steph who had lost her dad. I knew the interaction would be moving and meaningful, but I didn't think it would actually be her. I clicked over to her

Facebook wall and saw that her friends were already celebrating, tagging each other and sharing the link to my letter.

It took me a minute to decide how I felt about it. I was glad she had friends sharing this with her, but in a way it made it harder for me. They were calling me into the conversation, and I was worried that my careful words designed to make her feel loved and important would eventually be understood to say "You aren't the 'real' Steph." In fact, that was the most likely outcome.

She posted a note to me that said, in part:

Matt, I think I've cried a million tears today . . . I read your letter 50 times! THIS IS MINE!! I wrote this for my dad! Words cannot express what I am feeling right now. I have so much gratitude, peace, happiness, excitement in my heart right now! I bought this as a donation for a charity. It was quite a while back. Unfortunately I was not able to set this off in the sky. I paid for it and wrote on it, I continued about with my life, never expecting this to come back around . . . You have touched my life and lifted my spirit to a place that only my father could. I can't deny the miracle in this. I have never been a believer in anything of this sort. There are way too many things that had to happen to get this message back to me. I truly believe my dad worked through you to get this back to me. I don't care who believes me. None of that matters to me. What matters is how I feel, right here, right now. I know this is mine. How you got it is the mystery. I live in Salt Lake City, I'm very curious how it made it that far. I researched how far these things can go, which makes it that much more intriguing to me. There is a really cool backstory to all of this and I would love to share it with you. I sent you a Facebook message. I included my phone number. I hope to hear from you, Matt.

I was tired. I had been fielding notes about the lantern for almost two weeks. The thought of interacting with this woman, of actually talking to her on the phone . . . well, I knew that I should, I knew it would be good for her and probably for me, but I didn't feel that same excitement. I wasn't jumping up and down about it, especially because I knew it almost certainly wasn't her. How could the lantern fly all the way from Salt Lake City to my house? It was a two-day journey by car. I couldn't imagine how long it would take for the lantern to get here. I couldn't see how it would fight the winds and land at my feet.

She followed up with a second note. "By the way, was there something else written on that lantern? Because there's something else I always write." She shared what would have been written on it, if she had written it.

It was the exact thing that had been on my lantern. A little phrase I hadn't mentioned to anyone, not even my wife. And there it was, staring back at me from my e-mail.

So maybe this was the real Steph after all.

11

Promises

Her father had always promised to take her to New Mexico to see the hot-air balloons lifting off. He had shown her a picture. It was him facing the camera with a series of balloons rising, lifting from the ground and heading toward the heavens behind him in the distance, gently rising up and out of the frame.

Steph and I had been texting back and forth for a while. That day, for the first time, I had called her. I was driving home from work, talking while driving. After we said hello and sort of introduced ourselves, she told me how much she missed her dad and how grateful she was for the blog post, how much those reassurances meant to her, what a strange event had brought us to the point of being on the phone with each other, even though we were strangers. We chatted about our children—she has two boys—and I told her about Krista and our kids. We fell into an easy, comfortable brother-sister sort of relationship from our first phone call. I was relieved that she wasn't looking for a replacement father figure, and since she was only five years younger than me, a sibling friendship made a lot more sense.

I asked her where she had been when she sent the lantern. I had a hard time believing the little paper lantern had somehow traveled 770 miles, over mountains, through different sorts of weather, and landed at my house. It took a plane almost two hours to make the flight; it was a twelve-hour drive. I couldn't imagine a thin paper lantern with a small fuel cell making that journey. And yet, somehow it had.

She had been at a charity event toward the end of October called "Howlin' with the Angels." She was with her friend Sarah, and because it was a Halloween fund-raiser, they were both dressed as Pan Am flight attendants. Howlin' with the Angels was raising money for two charities: one called Angel's Hands Foundation, an organization dedicated to helping children with rare diseases have the highest possible quality of life, and a second called Children and the Earth, an organization to help disadvantaged kids.

There was a live band, and dinner, and hors d'oeuvres and a casino. Blackjack and roulette, dancing, a Texas Hold 'Em tournament. And in a hallway just outside the main meeting room, a long table that held large rectangles of paper. The people behind the table said they were sky lanterns: for a ten-dollar donation you could write something on the paper. The lanterns would be released at a later date.

They reminded Steph of her father's promise to take her to see the hot-air balloons. Steph handed over her ten dollars and wrote on the paper. "Love you, Dad. Miss you so much." Then one of her friends shouted at her to hurry up. They were about to get in the line for food and it was moving fast, so Steph quickly scribbled a heart with her name and one more line of text and went off to join the party. She didn't know when or where the lanterns had been sent. I wondered if maybe, for some reason, they had been launched a little closer to my house than Salt Lake City.

Later, I studied the weather maps. The prevailing winds always seemed to blow east, the opposite direction needed to bring a lantern to me from Utah. The jet stream also seemed to blow hard and fast in the wrong direction. The distance seemed incredible. Then again, I found several stories of people discovering balloons and lanterns released far from them.

It was still hard to believe that it had managed to get from her to me. Maybe it had hit the front of a Mack truck and been driven the rest of the way across the country, blowing into my yard like trash often did. Okay, that seemed unlikely, but it had come here somehow, and I was having trouble imagining its exact route.

"I get the feeling," Steph said, "that you believe a lot of the same weird stuff as my dad."

Her father, Roberto F. Aragón, had passed away a couple of years before. He was a strong man, full of life, who loved to ride motorcycles, didn't shy away from a fight, and wasn't afraid to sweep his daughter into his arms.

He had been known as an advocate for those in need. At his funeral, people came from all over the Salt Lake City area. Back in the day he had been a protestor, a guy focused on social justice for everyone. He was mentioned in a book Steph owned, a book about Chicano activism. Her dad was specifically mentioned as a friend the author enjoyed debating.

Roberto was born in 1951 in Tooele, near Salt Lake City. He lived three doors down from her mom, Marcella, as a kid.

They met in the neighborhood and married young. He was briefly in the military and was stationed in Germany.

He loved science fiction—loved watching terrible science fiction movies and reading the old pulp fiction novels. He loved his brother, "Kiko," and they enjoyed riding motor-cycles together. He loved his kids: Marty, Danny, Jesús, and Stephanie.

He had left when she was one. Her grandparents, aunt, and extended family played big parts in taking care of Steph while she was growing up. She went to see Roberto most summers into her teens, and he sent letters and would call from time to time. He came home for weddings. When Steph was twenty years old, he moved back to Tooele.

He never did take her to see the hot-air balloons. He brought it up every once in a while, but by then Steph was married with kids. It wasn't that she didn't want to go—she did. And it wasn't that he didn't plan to take her. It was just that life seemed to get in the way: there was always work to be considered, or the family needed something, or the dates of the hot-air balloon festival fell at the wrong time.

Roberto's liver eventually failed. Steph had gone to be with him for a week. He had been moved from the hospital to his home. He was dying. He knew it and Steph knew it. Her brothers, her mom, her uncle—everyone knew he was in his final days. That week was Steph's week to be with him and say good-bye.

They were watching television. He was stuck in his bed, so what else was there to do? The only things they could do were watch television, talk, and wait for the end. One of those terrible pseudo-documentaries was on, some show that purported to explore the afterlife, and Roberto was sharing his theories, thoughts, and ideas of what would happen on the other side.

He was Catholic. Steph had been Catholic once, baptized in the Church. But she wasn't Catholic anymore. She told me again how moved she had been by my letter. She had read it eighty times, she said. Now, talking on the phone, learning that I loved science fiction and had spiritual ideas that were similar to her father's, she was starting to get weirded out.

"Do you think there's a God?" she asked me.

"Steph," I said, "if there's a God, He's a father God. He made us and all the things I wrote in that letter about a good father—that he loves you, that he's proud of you, that he wants good things for your life—all those things are true of God's feelings for you, too."

Steph told me about the week she spent with her dad. She took time off work and spent every day with him, talking with him, watching television, arguing, sitting bored, or laughing about the past. There was one conversation that kept coming back to her as we talked about the impossibility of the sky lantern landing in my yard. They were watching that documentary, the strange one about the afterlife and theories about what happens after we die. Her dad told her more about what he thought would happen and his own beliefs about life after death.

Steph listened to his theories, a combination of his own thoughts and Catholicism. She didn't agree, and one thing everyone knew was that her dad liked to argue. He thought it was fun. She was pushing back, disagreeing with him about what would happen when he passed away. She thought they were enjoying it, having fun arguing with each other.

"You don't have to worry, Dad," she said. "You fall asleep and then there's nothing. You're at peace. That's all." Death was the end. After that, only silence.

He got angry at that. Something about that concept, that idea, hit against his core beliefs. The barriers between this life and the next were thinner than she thought, he claimed. "If there's a way to show you," he said, his dark eyes burning with a fierce intensity, "I'll contact you from the other side. I'll show you there is life after death."

It was a promise he seemed determined to keep.

12

Boarding

Steph and I had been in touch for several months (mostly through texts, but with an occasional phone call or e-mail), when I let her know that Krista and I were thinking of coming to visit. The whole experience had been so strange and interesting and life changing for me, I wanted to share it with others. So I'd been working on putting together this book, which Steph knew already.

My parents often take the kids for a week or so at a time

so Krista and I can travel together. But this particular week they were going to California, so Krista decided to stay home and take care of Myca, Zoey, and Allie. Krista often takes the kids by herself when I travel, and it's something I'm deeply thankful for. When she's away, I single-parent, too, but not as often as she does. The three of us were disappointed that Krista couldn't come to meet Steph—she told me to go and have fun and to be sure to send texts and pictures and to call every night. She even sent her camera along so I could take better pictures.

I've been in airports all over the world, but the Portland, Oregon, airport has to be one of the best. It's relatively small; you don't need a bus, train, trolley, or bicycle to get around. There is often live music, with musicians doing sets in the wide hallways between gates. There are actual restaurants with good food. The airport doesn't allow vendors to mark up prices just because they're behind security, so the prices are reasonable. The local independent bookstore, Powell's, has a location there, too. It's great to get local recommendations from a store owned and run in the area. I'll take whatever bookstore I can get, but I really love Powell's.

I parked in the economy lot and rode the bus to the airport. There were only three people in front of me at the security check: a dad with his two daughters. One was maybe eighteen months old, slung on his back like a baby monkey. The second was, I'm guessing, three years old. She was pulling a Dora the Explorer suitcase, and he was trying to explain the complicated Kabuki theater traditions of security protocol to her while simultaneously trying to keep her moving along. I told him I wasn't in any hurry, and he sagged with visible relief.

After passing through security, I wandered to the bookstore and browsed the science fiction and comics sections. I bought a cheeseburger for breakfast at Burgerville. I filled my water bottle. I realized I was nervous. I don't get nervous often—and I travel all the time—so it took me a few minutes, standing there eating my Tillamook cheeseburger (even the fast food is local and uses the nearby Tillamook dairy) with extra pickles, to figure out what was going on.

I was on my way to meet a woman who had lost her dad and who felt that her dad had spoken to her through my letter. Our interactions online and over the phone had been great . . . really wonderful, actually. She was sweet and kind and overflowing with positive things to say, and she wanted so badly to tell me about her life, and her dad, and what had happened as a result of the letter. She wanted to talk about the sky lantern and how it had flown so far and come to me. She wanted . . . well, I wasn't sure what she wanted, not completely. I couldn't help but think she wanted a life-changing moment in our two days together. Which, maybe, was why I was nervous.

I was worried I would disappoint her.

I stood there staring at the airport carpet. That carpet had been put down almost thirty years earlier; it was nearly as old as I was. You could tell. It was an almost aquamarine color, with deep-blue uneven-armed crosses. Small purple and red squares radiated out from there, and then the pattern repeated a hundred thousand times as it covered the fourteen acres of walkways and corridors throughout the airport. It looked like an '80s music video had laid down and died, right there on the airport floor, and someone had stapled it to the ground.

The airport had recently announced that they would replace the carpet, an announcement that was met with cries of outrage. An art project was started in which mosaics and quilts were made using scraps of the carpet. A "tweet your feet" campaign popped up, in which you were encouraged to take a picture of your feet before you flew—with that garish '80s background—and post it on social media. I have a friend who drove to the airport one day just to take her picture with the carpet before they tore it up. Gift shops sold socks and shirts with the pattern on them. A local magazine wrote a poem about it and began to write historical remembrances.

We can't even deal with an old carpet being replaced. How are we supposed to deal with the loss of a loved one?

I found my gate and sat on an uneven black chair that was connected to three others. It wobbled when I sat down, but it didn't matter. Steph and I had set up the trip and agreed to spend some time together, but as I was sitting there waiting to board the plane, I realized we hadn't said much other than "We'll meet each other." We hadn't made any plans. The trip was a bit last-minute, and she would have to work during the day, and I would be working and writing as well. We had decided to play things by ear.

I took my phone out. I should let her know I was on the way, at least. Let her know that all was going smoothly and I would see her soon.

My last text from her said, "I have a weird story to tell you. Lots to talk about."

I had no idea what that could mean. I would find out tonight, I supposed.

I thumbed in a quick message to her: "Hey there. I'm sitting at the airport waiting for my flight. Looking forward to meeting you today. Can I take you to dinner? Glad to hang out before and/or after also." I added a smiley face. Say what you want about emoji and smiley faces and the death of proper English and grammar (and believe me, I'll gladly say all those things: I used to be a high school English teacher), but one thing smiley faces do is tell people the mood you're in or how they should translate the tone of your texts.

I got a text back from her almost immediately. "Yes! I'm so excited to meet you I hardly slept." Four smiley faces. Four! "Let me know when you get settled in. I'll go meet up with you. I'm pretty free today. If you get lost or need me at all, just let me know. I can leave whenever. Let's plan on dinner for sure! If you drink coffee we can do that as well when you get here. Let me know. . . ." And, for good measure, a fifth smiley face.

She was so excited. I was looking forward to it, but she seemed almost giddy. I knew she had taken my words in the letter to heart, that she had taken them and held them in a deep, personal way. She had told me once that she had read the letter ten times in a row. It was startling, in a way. When she told me that, I wished I had spent more time writing the letter, a little more time getting the words precisely right.

I could see the potential for regret in this trip. What if I didn't say the right things? What if, instead of being life changing, it was a huge disappointment for Steph? What if I got back home and wished I had done things differently, had been more attentive, had spent more time with her, or said things more clearly? It was hard to deny that us getting together brought with it some expectation that she would be able to connect better with her dad.

In a small way, my feelings reminded me of my friend who had lost her sister in a plane crash. It was a sudden, unexpected, world-shattering devastation to her family. I don't know if she and her sister had fought the day she left. My friend doesn't like to talk about it. But she doesn't let her kids or her husband leave the house if they are angry at each other. It's a family rule. You leave the house having said everything you would want to say if you were never to see each other again. You don't walk out that front door without stopping to say "I love you" to every person in the house. That's how I was feeling. I wanted to make sure I said everything I wanted to say to Steph in those two days, but I also wasn't sure what I wanted to say. There was this feeling that we had a special connection, a bond that came from providence or coincidence or strange luck. But at the same time we'd never met. What if we didn't enjoy each other? What if the whole thing was awkward? What if we ran out of things to say?

I suddenly realized I hadn't said good-bye to Myca. I had put her to bed the night before, scouring the house for her stuffed unicorn, Uni. I dutifully propped her giant stuffed rabbit, Big Bunny, against the wall by Myca's head and tucked her little hummingbird into her arms. I read her stories, prayed for her, and turned out the light when she told me she was ready. But I didn't tell her I would be gone. Then, this morning, I left to catch my plane ten minutes before the kids woke up, only to find myself waiting at the gate forty minutes early.

I should have waited ten minutes and said good-bye.

Last night I had walked from the living room to the kitchen to go do some dishes. Krista and the older girls were watching a singing competition on television. As I walked by the couch, Allie stretched out from the couch like a cat, holding her arms out to me, wordlessly asking for a hug. I told her I'd be back in a minute, but I wanted to get the dishes done before the commercials were over.

I should have taken fifteen seconds to give her a hug.

Toward the end of the show Zoey had started telling me about a school project that she had helped write that she would be acting in. It was a play, an adaptation, really, of the "Little Mermaid" story, retold as a cautionary tale for dumb humans who thought they could become mermaids. It was called "The Little Cowgirl," and Zoey wanted to tell me the plot again, which she had done several times already. While it had been funny the first time, this time I let the words wash over me and didn't pay much attention, even though she clearly was proud of her accomplishment and wanted me to say "Good job!"

I should have looked her in the eye. I should have listened again.

If my plane went down today, God forbid, those imagined wounds wouldn't destroy my children. I had told Myca I loved her and given her a good-night hug. I gave Allie a hug before she went to bed. I printed off Zoey's "Little Cowgirl" for her that night. But I could have done more, been more present. These little regrets pile up, waiting for their moment to stab you in the heart.

I texted Steph. "I feel a little nervous. It's like meeting an old friend for the first time." Smiley face. I was addicted to smiley faces!

Steph's text came back. "Haha don't be nervous. I'm the one that should be nervous and I'm not at all." Smiley face with sunglasses on! That was a new one. She followed it up with "#Itwillbefunshesaid."

"I'm only a little bit nervous," I said. "I know we're going to have a great time."

"We will."

The gate attendant called for my row to board.

I slung my backpack on. I started toward the gate, then paused and looked down at my feet. I debated whether to take a picture, and finally decided the plane could wait another twenty seconds.

The picture was of my sneakers, two gray skate shoes standing on the edge of that dumb, beloved '80s carpet, like some weird art project where an everyday object is framed by the psychedelic background and you have no idea what might happen next. I had never noticed before, but the pattern wasn't a strange cross—it was intersecting runways. It was the Portland airport as seen from the air. It was a symbol of going places, or returning from them.

I boarded the plane and settled into my seat. I got one more text before I turned off my phone. A smiley face.

13

Face-to-Face

STEPH WAS ON HER WAY TO PICK ME UP. SHE WORKED FOR
an agency that set up housing for traveling executives, so
she had scored a place for me. It was a one-bedroom apartment, nicely decorated, a photo of Utah in winter on the
wall. It was in walking distance of a grocery store, a few restaurants, and a bookstore. When she knocked on the door,
I didn't quite run to answer, but I took big, fast steps. All
the nervous energy dissipated and a smile surfaced as my

hand hit the knob. I pulled the door open and there was an empty hallway.

For a split second I didn't know what had happened, and then Steph leapt out from the side of the door, like a kid hiding around the corner. I laughed and hugged her, and we were both saying how glad we were to finally meet.

She had come directly from work. Her car was a silver Audi, and when she turned the key, reggae blared so loudly that her hand shot out to turn it down. She pulled into traffic and we debated where we might go to eat while Bob Marley sang in the background.

"Let's go somewhere special," I said. "It's not every day you meet a friend for the first time."

"What kind of food do you like?"

"All kinds. But let's go somewhere you like. Not a cheap diner."

She laughed. "Well, shoot, that's what I like."

"Not Denny's," I said firmly.

"There's this place, Faustina. I like to go there for my birthday."

She promptly got us lost. She knew the town well, but we were both distracted, talking about how strange it was to be together, how weird that we had met through her sending that sky lantern. She told me she was glad I wasn't a serial killer. I told her the same. She apologized profusely for getting us lost, and meanwhile we turned in circles, as if the streets formed an enormous mandala. Maybe they did. Maybe our journey to the restaurant was a ritual tracing our own sacred space.

We sat at an outside patio beneath a Japanese maple, the red feathered leaves forming a canopy over us. The tree created a quiet space that felt comforting and private. We didn't hear the conversations of others or cars going by on the street. The air was cool and pleasant.

It didn't feel weird. There was a strange connection, a sudden comfort that came when we met. It didn't feel like a blind date, despite the fact that we were going to a nice dinner at a special restaurant. It didn't feel like some weird father-daughter thing, which was a relief. It almost felt like getting together with an old friend who you haven't seen for a long time. Like, maybe you were friends in high school—good friends—but you had drifted apart and now you were grabbing a meal and knew almost nothing about each other's lives. There was still a freedom to be yourself—an assumption that the other person liked you and was interested in what you had to say.

At the same time, we were learning strange little things about each other. For instance, Steph was allergic to chicken, turkey, beans, and avocados. "I'm the worst Spanish person ever." Her mom had made chicken soup a lot when Steph was little and she told her mom that it hurt when she swallowed. Her mom (like any mom) told her to stop complaining and trying to get out of it and to eat her soup.

"How did you finally figure out you were allergic, then?" I asked.

"I don't know. Anaphylactic shock, I think."

We split a Caesar salad. Steph ordered the salmon, pronouncing the *l* hard, as in *salmonella*. I got the lamb chops, which were amazing.

We talked about our kids (she has two sons, ages nineteen and sixteen, who she loves with a fierce protectiveness), about work, food, our relationships. We passed on dessert. She was too full and I was too picky.

"That letter—you don't even know . . . It changed my life," she said.

"It was amazing that we found each other."

"I was reading my tablet in bed that morning," she said. "I saw that sky lantern article at the top of my feed and I scrolled past it. But every time my page refreshed, it would be at the top again. So I finally clicked on it and started reading it—"

"What did you say? What was the first thing you said?"

"I started shouting, over and over. I jumped out of bed and started shouting at my boyfriend and my two boys, 'This is my lantern!' "

I laughed. "What did they say?"

"The boys were, like, 'Okay, whatever, Mom, it's your lantern.' My boyfriend wanted me to calm down and stop jumping. I showed it around that day and my friends asked if I was going to send you a note, but I said no, you probably had lots of people writing you and saying things, and I was just happy that you found it and I was reading the letter over and over and that was enough for me."

She had found the letter on a website that had republished it without my permission and not put any of my contact information on there. I had even written and asked them to either add a link to my info or take the letter down, and they hadn't. They hadn't even replied. All my bad feelings toward them evaporated now that I realized their website had brought me to Steph.

She specifically told her friends she wasn't going to try to find me. One of her friends decided that he would do the heavy lifting of searching me out, which, given my last name, hopefully was about ten seconds of typing and clicking on a search engine. He had been the one to send me a note saying "We found Steph for you" that first week in December.

Hearing the story from Steph's point of view made me a little sad. She said she had written me, and all her friends wanted to know if I had written back. Her mom wanted to know what I had to say. Steph kept saying I hadn't written back right away, and I wondered how long it had taken me. Certainly not longer than a day or two. I'm sure I sent a politely worded note about being glad she felt connected to her dad, and I hoped she had found some peace, just as I had done with the other Stephs.

When her mom asked her again if I had written back, she said, with obvious disappointment, "Yeah. He didn't really say much" and that I hadn't seemed excited and seemed not to realize what a big deal this was. She was right. I didn't know she was the one who had sent the sky lantern at that point. I had thought my polite notes to these women had come across as kind and caring, but, listening to Steph, I thought I might have seemed cold given how excited they were, how much they wanted me to write back and say, "This is amazing! I'm so glad I found you!"

I told her about the "other" Stephs (and the one Sherri) who had written to say it was their sky lantern, and how I was trying to be kind and loving without telling them all that I thought the lantern I found was the same one they had sent. That made sense to her. She said she had been staring at the lantern picture and wondering if it had said anything else on it, because she knew it had said one more thing on hers.

So she wrote me and asked.

And it did.

And now here I was.

I told her I was glad she had written again and had taken one more risk by sending me a note and asking that question instead of walking away disappointed and never writing again.

"I'm glad, too," she said. "Otherwise you might be hanging out with Sherri right now."

We both laughed at that. We took a picture beneath the Japanese maple.

Later that night she told me, "Seriously, that letter changed my life."

"Changed it how?"

"I made a list," she said.

"A list of what?"

"Of all the ways I was going to change my life. I'm working through the list now."

"Can I see it?"

"Yes," she said. "It's on my door at work. I'll show you tomorrow."

We kept talking that night. She had brought some old photographs of her dad, his dog tags, a couple of books he loved, some letters he had written. We looked at them, talked about her dad, talked about her, talked about her kids.

After Steph left, I called Krista and we talked about our days. She told me about how she and the kids were doing, and I filled her in on the time I had spent with Steph. "You would like her," I said. "She's looking forward to meeting you this summer."

"Great," Krista said. "That should be fun.

"The kids and I miss you," she said.

"I miss you guys, too."

We said good night and I prayed for her, Allie, Myca, and Zoey. Then I lay in the dark of my unfamiliar room and wondered what it would be like for my kids, how much they would miss me if I were gone not just for a few days but forever. I wondered what it was like for Steph, to miss her dad for the rest of her life . . . what questions she had for him, and what she wished he could say to her. She probably had questions for her dad. I thought I might ask her about that the next day.

14

A Tent

"I ALWAYS WONDERED IF MY DAD WAS PROUD OF ME," Steph said.

He had wanted her to be a lawyer. He had wanted to be a lawyer himself—he saw the law as a way to bring justice to those in need. Everyone said he was always looking out for those who needed help, needed protection, needed an advocate. He wanted that life for Steph, for her to be the one who would stand up for others, to be a strong woman who saw the weak and helpless and provided for them, protected them.

One summer day in August, just weeks before her sophomore year of high school would begin, Steph discovered she was pregnant. Her boyfriend (soon to be husband) was eighteen. She was the youngest child, the only daughter in her family. Her dad had moved away fifteen years before and had become a sort of irregular ghost, arriving in unexpected letters, phone calls, and occasional glorious moments in person.

He sent a letter.

It said, in part:

Dear Stephanie,

Just these few lines to say hi and let you know I am thinking of you. I hope and pray this letter finds you in all the best of health and in the good graces of God the Father.

Mi hitia, I heard of your situation. All I can say is if there is anything I can do, let me know. I don't guess I can do too much from here but I won't be here forever. Always remember, I love you no matter what happens. You are my baby girl. It won't matter how old you are.

How do you feel? What do you think about your situation, mi hitia?

I wanted to start writing to you before now but never took the time. I am sorry for that. I hope you will write back soon. Baby, you're a young woman now, don't be afraid to write or state your mind ever.

Stephanie, you must know, no matter what, your mom and I are there. I know I am not there physically, but you can know in your heart I am with you in spirit.

So when are you due? What are you hoping for? Mi hitia, I'll pray for a healthy baby, something we do a lot around here is pray.

Well, Steph, I need to go for now. Write soon. Tell your mom I said write me a letter with her thoughts soon so I can write her back.

Love,

Your Dad,

Roberto F. Aragón

I understood why Steph might wonder if her dad was proud of her. She didn't become a lawyer—never got a law degree. She skipped out of high school in the twelfth grade, but came back and finished later. She married Danny, who joined the military, and they found themselves living in Cheyenne, Wyoming, far from their family and friends. Danny needed the car during the day, and she was home—just her and the baby.

When she showed me the letter from her dad, she had spread out a collection of things from him, a sort of treasure box of memories. There were pictures of her, her dad, her brothers, and other members of her family. She had a collection of old driver's licenses and ID cards. She even had her father's college diploma from the University of New Mexico.

She held a letter she had written her dad long ago. She had obviously been young—I'd guess seven or eight years old from the handwriting and crazy spelling. Her dad had torn the note in half at some point and only the top part remained.

"The bottom's a mystery," she said.

Her dad had carried the letter in his wallet. Steph got it back after he passed away.

"To Dad," it said. "I love you. This is your girl Stephanie. Sometimes I think about you. You are my favorite one in the family. But you are funny. You make me laugh. You are funny and you bit my fingers." Steph said he would always pick her up and say how chubby her fingers were and pretend to gnaw on them. It's something she has always remembered. Then she wrote, "This is to remind you that I love you," and then there were fragments of words and the frayed end of the paper.

What is it about us human creatures that we need to hear those words of affirmation—that we need to be reminded?

We need to be told we are loved, not just remember that someone said it once upon a time. Maybe we're worried that something has changed, and I guess sometimes it does. We wouldn't have so many divorces otherwise. It's easy to see how a child could think that if Mom and Dad stopped loving each other, maybe they could stop loving their child as well.

So we want to know not just that we *were* loved but that we *are* loved. Roberto carried his daughter's sweet note in his wallet until the day he died, a reminder that there was a little girl once, somewhere in the world, who loved him. And Steph wondered, years later, if her father would have felt proud of her, despite her not having achieved all his educational goals for her, despite her not becoming a lawyer and changing the world.

I sat back in wonder that she could have the question. She's funny and kind and has made hard decisions in life. She cares for people around her: she hands money to homeless people when she walks by, she takes care of her boys, she's still in a relationship with her ex-husband, she connects with her extended family, she takes care of people.

I don't think there's any question her father would be proud of her.

She told me one story about being sixteen that made me know, without a doubt, that he should be proud.

Steph was in the hospital. She'd just given birth to her first son.

Her hospital room overlooked the city. She could see the lights against the darkness and see the distant evidence of life outside her room.

She was only a sophomore in high school.

When they tried to hand Steph the baby, she wouldn't take him—not the first day. She hadn't wanted to be pregnant and didn't want to hold him. She lay back in the bed, exhausted and wrung out, waving the nurses away, her hair plastered to her face. She turned and looked out the window.

As she looked, she remembered when she was eight years old and her dad had returned for her brother's wedding. He dedicated a song to her during the reception: "Daddy's Home." He danced with her and she cried. It was the first time she remembered feeling something like that—that deep emotion. She fell asleep in his arms that night. It was still one of her favorite memories.

The next day the nurses tried again. They brought the baby in, with his tiny face and dark hair, his minuscule fists wrapped up in the blanket, and she reached out for her son, took him in her arms, and pulled him against her chest.

She took a blanket and pulled it over her head, making a tent. It was just him and her now. There was no one else. She held him in the crook of her arm, the small, new warmth of him sinking into her. She rocked him in her makeshift tent and said over and over, "Dear God, don't let me hurt him. Dear God, don't let me mess up his life. Dear God, don't let me hurt him."

Sixteen years old, holding her baby, and in that moment she made a decision: she would rearrange her life around this one.

Who wouldn't be proud of a young woman like that?

What a beautiful moment. What a beautiful person.

And all the things her dad wanted for her: to stand up for others, to be a strong woman who saw the weak and helpless and provided for them, to be someone who protected others—did it really matter that she would do it for this tiny boy instead of for strangers? That she would do it as a mother instead of as a lawyer? No. Not at all.

Under that blanket, alone with her son, their breath mingling in that tiny space, Steph couldn't see the city or the life outside anymore. What was happening out there—none of that mattered. Everything that mattered was there in that tiny space. This was life. This was love. This was home.

15

Tooele

WE HAD DRIVEN OUT FROM SALT LAKE CITY AS THE SUN
was setting. Steph texted her aunt to see if she was around,
and we thought we'd go see Tooele, the town where she
had grown up. We rolled past the Great Salt Lake, both of
us laughing at the terrible smell. We passed a copper refin-
ery, too. Historically, the two biggest employers in Tooele
had been that copper mine and a chemical weapons disposal
plant, which got rid of chemical weapons like mustard gas,

sarin, and VX. It was a suburb for a reason, a liminal town on the edge of habitability. It was the last outpost of the desert. It was the borderland between life and death.

Late that night, long after dark, we went by the Tooele cemetery. Steph wasn't sure we would be able to find her dad's grave in the dark. She grinned. "You don't think there will be zombies, right?" She was pulling on her coat. Although it had been warm in the daytime, the temperature had dropped as fast as the sun.

"Zombies? No reason to be afraid of zombies. If it's werewolves, we're going to have a problem. I don't do werewolves."

I told her to be careful as we stepped onto the uneven grass field, because she was wearing heels. "Boots," she clarified. "I'm wearing boots." Then she made a joke about breaking her leg. I told her to be careful because I would, I swear, leave her for the werewolves.

We couldn't find the grave at first, and Steph held her phone up at face level, a small light in the darkness, and started to chant, "Where are you Dad? Where aaaaarrrrre youuuuuu?"

We passed several tombstones belonging to her family. They had lived in the town, one way or another, for three generations. I was struck by how young and recent some of the dead were. The family didn't have much of a choice when they first came here, many decades ago. There was a part of town called Tortilla Flats where Hispanics, Latinos, Mexicans, and anyone who spoke Spanish or had dark skin had been forced to live. That was home for them. We had driven through the neighborhood and Steph pointed out the window at her grandparents' most recent house, and then the houses where her mom and dad had grown up and eventually met each other—just a few small houses between them.

We found her dad's tombstone. Steph's name was written on the back, and the names of her brothers, too. It was startling to see that. There was space reserved for her there. A small black rectangle was attached to the back, evidence of his service in the Army. Her dad's tombstone included his name and the dates of his life on the front with his photo in the upper right corner. Engraved across the bottom half was a picture of him riding his motorcycle.

I took a few pictures of the gravestone and Steph there beside it. We didn't hear a voice or feel his presence, or at least I didn't. I knelt beside her in the grass and put my hand on her shoulder.

She said, "This is weird, right?"

"Yeah," I said. "It's weird."

The next stone over was that of her nephew, dead at seventeen. He had been a beloved football star in town. Her family is haunted by his death, questioning if they could have done anything differently, if other choices might have prevented his loss. Looking at his gravestone, I could see how much this young man was worth to this family, how deeply they loved him, and how they would trade anything for a few more years with him.

We drove all over the town that night. Sometimes I could hear the anger creep into her voice. We started with the local burger joint everyone loved, then the hospital where she and her dad had been born, a tiny place that was also, oddly, a retirement home. She would talk about how there was nothing to do in Tooele, how the highlight of her high school years was climbing to the top of a nearby mountain. The city had put a giant cement T for Tooele on the mountain, and it had become a senior tradition to hike up there and light signal flares on it. She talked about how heroin use had risen in the town and was eating its way through the young people. How her best friend had died right here, on this stretch of road, along with her friend's infant child, because of an accident caused by a drugged-up driver.

That was the final straw. That's when she knew her boys couldn't grow up there, even though she knew they would never do drugs. She made them promise never to touch drugs.

This was her town. Her heritage. Her family. Slowly dying, slowly moving from the tiny hospital to the wide graveyard down the street.

We stopped to see her aunt Geneil, a woman who had been a central loving presence in her life in a place that wasn't easy to grow up in. One of her best friends, Steph said. Aunt Geneil was a small woman who made her way through the shadows of the foyer to the front door and let us in. We followed her into a bright room bordered with bookshelves. Small plastic models of hot-air balloons were attached to one wall. A poster of one of her sons, a professional magician, was on the mantel.

Aunt Geneil sat on her chair, a small dog curled up beside her. We talked about life, her kids, and the family she and Steph shared. Tragedy, comedy, history, and soap opera all rolled into one. Steph kept apologizing for her crazy family as we talked, and I was struck by the fact that it wasn't crazy at all. It seemed like the story of every family, if you went deep enough. No one has that perfect sitcom family. We all have unresolved problems, tensions, questions, and histories. It might not be what shows up on the annual Christmas card, but it's what happens in the thirty seconds before the photographer presses the button.

Steph wondered if her aunt could tell us some more

stories about Steph's dad. Steph knew precious few. "Do you know any stories about my dad?" she asked. "People always tell me he was an activist, that he did so many things to help people. Do you know those stories?"

Her aunt was quiet. Awkwardly silent.

"Those stories? I don't know any of those."

"How about any kind of story?"

"You know how I feel about your dad."

As soon as she said the words, I knew how she felt about him. Here was Steph, deeply devoted to the memory of a man who had loved her but in many ways hadn't lived up to that love.

"My aunt thinks my dad shouldn't have left me," Steph said to me, as if this was absurd. Because she knew her dad was amazing, knew he was a good man and a good dad.

There were so many ways this conversation wasn't my business, but in the last forty-eight hours I had come to consider Steph not just a friend but a good friend, like a sister. How could we share so many things about our lives and have that not be true? We had been honest with each other so far, and there was no reason to stop now. I said, "I think what your aunt is saying is that, while your dad was there for you and loved you, your life might have been different if he had stayed and been here for you even more. He was a good dad, but his effect on your life might have been stronger if he had stayed."

Steph started to tell us in protest that everyone had loved her dad and that he had been a good man—how all of those people had come to his funeral and how respected he had been. And all those things were true. She was so thankful for the little bit she had from him, and I have no doubt—not the slightest—that he had loved her deeply. But it was like she couldn't see, couldn't admit, that he could have done better by her.

I had a sudden insight that the reason Steph had put up with so much garbage in her life was because she didn't realize her own value. She had been a wife or girlfriend, a mother and dutiful daughter, since she was sixteen.

Steph had been told her whole life that she wasn't worth much. She wouldn't say that, but I could feel it in the air of that town. Her family had been told for generations where to live to keep them out of sight of the rich folks. Her dad had left her behind, making time for her in the summers, sending letters and phone calls, but was largely absent all the same. This town, flooded with heroin, was rotting the core of the community in exchange for wads of cash. The chemical disposal plant offered people a job risking their lives in exchange for twenty-five dollars an hour. As near as I can tell from my research online, there were lines of people hoping for a job despite the risks.

Twenty-five dollars an hour in exchange for getting rid of things like mustard gas, weapons made decades ago, their toxic aftereffects seeping down through the generations, coming here to this town, lurking in the background of its residents' lives. Children were paying the price for the decisions made by their parents, their grandparents, their great-grandparents without knowing that the destructive choices they made in their own lives would reverberate down through the years to their own children's children.

I felt the anger now.

Anger that this amazing woman didn't know what she is worth. That she would accept less than she deserved in relationships because she thought it was the best she could expect. Anger that the first time people like Steph might really understand how much the people around her love her—the first time she might be able to fully accept her value—might be when they lavishly decorate her tombstone, weeping and speaking the honest, loving words about her life.

That Tooele chemical plant kept flashing into my mind. It was the perfect metaphor for a town like this. People take the job and risk the damage because twenty-five dollars an hour is worth it. Right?

"You deserve better," I said. "A lot of things you're doing in life are because you don't think you deserve better. You don't think you're worth more. And because you're not putting the right value on yourself, you're not making choices that take into account how much you're worth. Steph, you are worth so much more than you know. You deserve better. You need to demand it."

Her aunt said, "See?" She had been telling Steph this for years.

I got some tissues from her aunt's table. Steph dabbed at her eyes. I told her I hadn't meant to make her cry. We talked awhile longer, then said good-night to her aunt and her dog.

On the way home, Steph opened up even more about her current troubles. She told me some things about a group of her friends, about decisions she had made that she feared would take her down a dark path.

We talked about life, God, children, parents, being a parent, self-worth, being loved, and how to find a good path when you feel lost—when you know how you got there but not how to get out.

She cried and I listened, I asked questions, I shared my thoughts. I asked if I could pray for her before she left, and she said yes. So I did.

After I got back to my room, I called Krista and processed

the whole night . . . how the town reflected Steph's life in many ways. Steph was, like so many people, a wonderful person who was kind, generous, thoughtful of others, and also grieving and, at least sometimes, in pain. I told Krista about the visit to Steph's aunt, the graveyard, the whole thing. It was amazing that this new friendship had come about because of the sky lantern that had somehow landed in our yard. It was an honor to hear Steph's story and to take a moment to encourage her. It was a beautiful thing to realize that, in missing her father, she had reached out and we had become friends.

I was glad to be there for her, at least for a couple of days, to talk about the things she could no longer talk about with her dad. I was glad I had been given the chance to speak for him and to tell her that he loved her, that he was proud of her, that she was worthy of love.

"It's good that you're able to be there to talk about all these things," Krista said.

"I think so, too."

We said our good-nights, and I told her I would see her the next day. Tomorrow was my last day hanging out with Steph. I hung up the phone.

No one likes saying good-bye.

16

Farewells

WE WENT TO LUNCH AT PORCUPINE, A RESTAURANT AT the foot of ski country. Steph kept saying, "I can't believe how fast this has all gone. We should have gone up to Park City! We could still go, but we went in the opposite direction."

"This is great, though. You said it was your favorite place to eat."

"It snuck up on me. I wanted to do all these other things. I wanted you to meet both my boys, and my brothers at least. I wanted to do a family thing."

"This isn't the last time we'll see each other." We had talked about future plans the previous evening. I was driving through on my way to Colorado in June, and I'd stop at least to grab coffee or a meal. She was talking about bringing her boys out to Portland so she could hang out with Krista and the girls.

"Have I told you how happy I am that you're here?" she asked.

This was a joke between us now. She must have said it several times yesterday. "Not a single time," I said.

We took our seats on a balcony overlooking the rest of the restaurant, ordered our food, and talked, mostly about our kids. "There are certain people who change your life forever," Steph said. She was talking about her sons. They had saved her life. "When the rest of my friends were getting into drinking and drugs, I was taking care of my sons."

We talked for a while about how we all wanted to hear one more time that we were loved, that our parents were proud of us. We talked about how to make sure our own kids understood that we loved them.

Steph is good at this, letting people know how she feels about them.

The night before, she had given me a gift with a letter. "Is this a crystal ball?" I had asked, unwrapping a small sphere.

"No," she said.

I laughed because it was definitely a ball and looked like crystal to me. "Quartz?"

"I wrote down what it is," she said. "I can't remember. Someone told me it would help if you got writer's block."

I turned it in my hand. I didn't think it would solve my writing problems, but it was beautiful. When I turned the ball in my hand I could see what looked like clear spots, but they would go foggy again if I turned it or held it up to my eye. It was smooth, but inside there were cracks that formed internal chambers. I could see colors snaking through it to the other side. I told her it was beautiful, and thanked her for the gift.

She also gave me a card. I wasn't allowed to read it yet, she said. I had to wait until I got back to the apartment, later that night. The envelope was light brown, made from recycled paper. A decorative white rectangle was on the front, and she had addressed it to "My Saving Grace . . ."

The card had gold-stamped flowers, with watercolor trees in the background, and gold and purple triangles washed above, coming down like rays of light. A feather floated toward the top of the scene, and below it was written, "The Answer Is Blowing in the Wind." Steph had written across the top, "Fly little Sky Lantern!!"

Her letter said, in part:

Matt,

My newfound friend, thank you for visiting me, your time, the letter, your friendship. I have so much gratitude in my heart. It has been a nice visit so far, all of the nervous feelings were for nothing.

I hope we stay in touch. Your letter changed my life. It seems so silly, but it's true. You have a gift, Matt, I'm glad to see you put it to good use and help people like me, who at times feel lost. I've had a lot of loss and pain in my life. I try to stay optimistic. It is hard, though . . . I must stay strong for my two boys, who are my world. I want to show them that giving up is not an option. Your letter gave me my faith back. I know my dad watches over me daily, your letter solidified that for me.

I hope from all of this, always remember you changed at least one person's life. This is your masterpiece, and I feel so lucky to have witnessed your glory days.

I hope you continue to be blessed in love and life. You have a beautiful family. You are a wonderful dad. Always show your girls how a man should treat them, to be confident and kind but don't take garbage from anyone.

I'll miss you. I hope you and your family come visit. I
would love to meet them, tell them thank you for letting me
visit with you. I missed my dad when he was away!
Thank you for my letter!

Always Love, Respectfully,

Stephanie

I hadn't told her thank you for the card yet, so I told her over lunch. Then we went down the mountain, back to her office.

It was a small but neat office. I sat in the chair across from her desk. She had a small shelf of souvenirs and decorations. On the back of her office door she had a list of goals for the year.

"I made that after reading your letter," she said. "I knew I had to change my life."

There was a series of goals: selling a certain amount at work, paying off some debt, finding someone who would love her the way she deserved to be loved.

On the shelf of knickknacks was the picture of her dad with the hot-air balloons. He was wearing a poncho and facing the camera, not exactly smiling, but with a satisfied look on his face.

"I used to stare at that photo for hours," Steph said. "The first time he showed me that picture, I told him I wanted to go there. He said he would take me." She was silent for a moment. "He never did." She used to stare at the photo, imagining her dad taking her to New Mexico, going to see the hot-air balloons rise up, the baskets drifting low, the multicolored balloons filling the sky.

We chatted. Small talk, mostly. I met a couple of her friends. We wandered to a church coffee shop across the parking lot, then wandered back. We had too much to say and no time left to say it.

I needed to pack my things and get to the airport. "I should probably go," I said.

She nodded, sitting behind her desk, not looking at me.

"Are you okay?" I asked. "Are you feeling sad?"

"I'm okay," she said, and the first tears slid down her cheeks.

I went over to her, sat on the desk in front of her, and took her right hand in mine. "This isn't the last time we'll see each other," I said.

But we don't know that, do we? We never do. We look into the future and things seem clear, but the crystal turns and it is foggy again. Things that seemed certain never happen, unexpected changes come upon us, altering our lives in an instant.

She stood up and we hugged. "I love you, Steph," I said.

"I love you," she said.

She walked me to my car, told me to stay in touch and to text from Portland.

I drove back to the apartment, surprised at how sad I felt. Surprised that this woman, who I barely knew, felt like an old friend and had become someone important to me. I found myself pausing while packing my clothes, standing beside the bed, just thinking about the last couple of days. I was sad to be leaving but glad to be headed back to see Krista and my own kids. My parents, both still alive. My many other friends. I felt sad, though, to leave Steph. I felt like I was taking away a closer connection to her dad.

I was sitting at my gate an hour later, thinking about my trip, which had come to an end much faster than I had expected. I had a new friend who lived a long way across the country. Someone I would have never met, would have never known, if not for that lantern crashing in my yard. I had driven through her city many times. She had come to visit Portland, even staying ten miles from my house.

It was strange to think that all the so-called strangers around me might be one small act of kindness away from becoming good friends. We have so much in common, all of us. We have lost our loved ones, or we will. We have lived, fought, loved, and wanted to be loved. We have cried and laughed, struggled in relationships. We have lit the darkness with our small flames. Is that not enough to build a friendship around?

What if Steph wasn't some amazing friend I had found through a series of inconceivable coincidences or generous providence? What if, instead, it was that every place was full of these potential friends, crowded around us, but we were unable to see them? Could it be that every person sitting here around me could be someone who would be my friend, if only I took a few moments? If only I gave them my full attention?

This crowd at the airport. A man sat across from me in a red tracksuit. At the window, a round man in an aloha shirt. A woman and her daughter sat next to me, the girl singing a song and watching the planes. The TSA officers. The woman who had printed out my boarding pass. The family in front of me in the security line, stopping to say good-bye to their father before going into the line, holding things up, slowing us down.

We're such short-lived creatures and yet the most important things about life are true for all of us: we have parents or had them, we fall in love, we want respect, we are beautiful, we lose things and people we love, and one day we, too, will go the way of those before us, in a never-ending procession from life into something else.

But we all go along our way, boarding the plane, not making eye contact, scanning our boarding passes, shoving carry-ons into the overhead bins, settling into our seats, buckling our seat belts, and jockeying for position on the armrests. We are going somewhere together, all of us, but despite all that, we don't know one another, don't take the risk to get to know one another, don't make the assumption that we could be something more than strangers on the same journey.

When the plane rose into the air, we entered a bank of low-hanging clouds. Below I could see the Great Salt Lake, water lapping against a low hill, the edges stark and white in the late sunlight. Then we moved through the clouds, and everything below was covered. A moment of clear, and then the fog.

17

Homecoming

I WALKED INTO THE HOUSE AT NINE THIRTY THAT NIGHT. Myca shouted "DAD!" from upstairs—two hours past her bedtime. Allie, still in her ballet leotard, slammed into my chest, followed by Zoey, who ended up with a half-Dad, half-Allie hug and then demanded her own once we untangled. Krista was playing bunko with some of our neighborhood friends and had left the older girls in charge.

Myca waited for me in the dark. I was impressed that she

had stayed in her bed when I came through the door, but she had been in bed a couple of hours at that point. I knelt down beside her bed and rubbed her back, told her hello, and gave her a kiss.

"A nightmare woke me up," she said.

"Oh, yeah? What kind?"

"The evil kind."

"Oh. That's not good."

"Like the kind about a slipper."

"A slipper?"

"A glass slipper."

"Cinderella?"

"Yeah. It was that evil nightmare about Cinderella. It had just started and then I woke up."

"Okay. Well, I'm here now. I'll pray for you and stay with you until you fall asleep again."

She cuddled deeper into her bed with a contented sigh and closed her eyes.

Kids don't come with instructions. It would be great to know little hints like not to show my youngest daughter Cinderella movies. Being afraid of a princess movie came as a bit of a surprise, because her whole life she's never been afraid of much of anything, especially not monsters. At Halloween she stands in the department store, bent over laughing at the eight-foot-tall ghouls you can buy for your front porch. She skips houses that aren't decorated with enough scary decorations. When she was two years old, she shouted to tell me there were monsters outside her window. I offered to close the shade and she told me no. She just wanted me to know they were out there. She thought I would be interested.

I tell new dads who are worried about their impending newborns to think about it like a video game: the skill set builds on itself. When your kid is born, you don't know how to do anything. Change a diaper. Feed the baby. Give them a bath. Nothing. About the time you start to figure it all out, the kid starts to crawl. Then to walk. It's all new levels, just like a video game. You figure out one level and then the next, more challenging level comes along.

I remember spending a whole day trying to childproof our house. I could barely use an electric drill and screwdriver. By the time I was done, even adults couldn't access the kitchen chemicals. If human children were like deer, we would be in trouble. Fawns are able to stand, walk, and run within hours of their birth. It would be pure chaos for the human parents: we'd never survive. But levels—we can do that.

As a kid you think your parents are destroying your life

on purpose, but the fact is, kids, we're destroying your lives completely by accident. We don't mean to do it. We're actually doing our best to provide you with a good life.

The parenting books, too, which I'm sure are wonderful for some people, drove me crazy. Zoey learned to escape from her crib early on. She would grab the top rail and vault over. I would hear a bone-shaking thump and then the sound of tiny feet pattering on the floor. I cannot tell you how terrifying it was the first time I was awoken in the night by a crash only to hear tiny feet making their way to my bed, and then for a three-foot tall creature to stand in the darkness just staring at me.

We couldn't get her to stay in bed; Krista and I tried everything. Every parenting technique you can imagine short of handcuffs. I bought a book purporting to help you control uncontrollable children. I locked myself in the bathroom, sitting fully clothed on the toilet, grumbling under my breath as some psychologist calmly explained how my intense child could be trained with consistency, patience, and firmness. It was like he didn't understand that I was sleep deprived and my child had somehow inherited an Olympian's vaulting skills.

I ended up sitting in the hallway each night. When Zoey's door opened, I would tell her no, pick her up, and set her back in her bed. A million times. Every night. Thank God she fell in love with books, because I would just pile them by her bed and she would lay there looking at pictures.

Was this good parenting? I honestly have no idea.

Allie came along and slept perfectly through the night. When she was two years old, she started coming up and telling us, right around bedtime, that she was tired and would someone please walk her to her bedroom and say good-night. Then she would close her eyes, take a deep sigh, and fall asleep.

Myca went through a phase when she slept in a cat bed, one of those foam ovals covered with a fuzzy outer sheath. We didn't even have a cat at the time, but she found it somewhere, curled up in it, and loved it. For years she couldn't sleep unless she had her "kitty bed." She would set it on top of her mattress, settle in, and go right to sleep. Sometimes she would meow first. When her body outgrew the cat bed, we seriously debated whether to upgrade to a doggy bed.

These are such little examples. Parents look at their children, trying to figure out what to do, trying to do our best to make our kids feel loved and to prepare them for the world. To help them be successful and survive one day without us. Of course we mess up. Often because we're afraid, tired, or angry.

One time we were driving in our van and Zoey was playing with a stick. She was maybe four years old. She loved the stick, I can't remember why, but I asked her to put it down because I was afraid if we were in an accident it would stab her. But she wouldn't put it down. I told her more strongly to put it down, and she wouldn't, and I got angry. I reached back, grabbed the stick, and flung it out the car window.

Krista looked at me with utter calm and said, "That seemed like a bit of an overreaction."

Yes. It was. Zoey was bawling. I instantly felt horrible. The story ended with me pulling over and walking down the road, trying to find the my daughter's stick.

So much of parenting comes down not to knowing the answers but knowing your child and knowing yourself. It takes time, and it takes a lot of commitment. It requires, essentially, taking on your kids as a sort of hobby. The easiest way to mess it up is to put your own desires over the needs of your kids.

Don't get me wrong, there are plenty of terrible parents out there. There are amazing parents who have terrible moments. There are absent parents who desperately love their kids, and there are parents who are present but ignore them.

I hope that most of us are stumbling through, doing our best. Knowing our kids, loving them, is an important first step. Letting our kids know and understand us—that's part of it, too.

After Myca was all settled into bed, I came downstairs to eat some dinner. Zoey was on the couch, writing a novel. Allie was curled up in a chair. Zoey asked if we could watch *Jurassic Park 3*. She has been on a dinosaur kick. Allie said no way and insisted we watch *Back to the Future*. They wanted me to make the final decision. I told them to flip on the cable and see what free movies were on.

The Matrix was available, and they had never seen it. The three of us sat on the couch, me in the middle, and I laughed at their questions about the movie. I remembered seeing it for the first time myself, and how I had walked out of the theater, mind blown, amazed by the movie. It was fun to see the same thing happening to them. I couldn't remember if I had seen it with Krista or with my brother, and I wondered out loud who it was.

"Your brother?" Zoey asked. "I think you mean your sister."

"What? No. My brother."

"You just said your 'brother' on accident, Dad." Allie was looking at me like I was crazy.

"I have a brother, you know," I said. He was my half brother, actually, but I've never liked the "half" terminology. My Chinese friends laughed when I used the term. "Half of a brother? Ha ha ha!" He hadn't been around much in the last decade or so, which made me sad, but I had told the kids about their uncle Ed more than once. Apparently when they were too young to remember.

"Are you joking right now?" Allie asked. "Because I can't tell."

"What? No!" I wandered upstairs and found the box with our wedding album, right on top of our bookshelf. I blew the dust off the book, heavy with years and memories, and returned downstairs. I sat between the girls and opened up the album to a picture of the family. Krista and me in the middle, my sisters on either side of us, my parents, and, there on the end, in his tuxedo, Ed. "There he is," I said.

"Huh," the kids said.

It seemed like a big miss that the kids didn't know about their uncle. I had told them before, I thought they knew. There are times when not letting kids know enough about yourself is the same as not letting them know about their own selves: why certain things are the way they are, what the reality of their own family is.

They curled in close to me. Krista came home from bunko. The movie was still playing. There was no school the next day, so bedtime was a little later. The movie wasn't over, and the kids grumbled, but when I said it was time for bed, they each hugged me and kissed my cheek. My older daughters made their way up the stairs into the bedroom they share, brushed their teeth, and tucked themselves in without complaint or argument or me sitting in the hall—without needing kitty beds, stuffed animals, songs, or story time to fall asleep.

They were growing up, and despite all the hand-wringing about getting them into bed when they were small, they seemed to be doing fine now. I decided to count that as a victory.

18

Geek Dad

"Why don't you ever write books for us?"

Zoey and Allie asked me this sometimes. To be funny, I would say, "Why don't you ever write books for *me?*"

My first book was published when they were nine and seven. It was about miscarriages, religion, suffering in the world, and whether God was good, powerful, and loving. It wasn't for children. My second book was about family, trying to become a good person, abuse, when to leave a marriage, and werewolves. Yes, werewolves. Also not for kids.

My kids saw me devote a lot of time to my writing. I would sit in the living room typing while the rest of the family watched television. I would lie in the hammock during the summer months, pounding out words while hanging over the grass. They wanted me to invest some of that time into them.

I had tried more than once to make them fall in love with the stories central to my own childhood. They never really took to *Star Wars*. I probably showed it to them when they were too young. Zoey was interested in Princess Leia, but the rest of the movie didn't hold her interest. Allie seemed to think it was a comedy. She laughed hysterically when Han Solo and Chewbacca burst into the prison guard room, Han throwing Chewie a blaster.

"Even the dog is fighting!"

"That's not a dog," I said. "That's a Wookiee, and his name is Chewbacca."

She started rolling on the floor, almost crying from laughter. "The dog's name is Chewbacca?"

I started Myca on samurai movies when she was a few months old. She didn't sleep well as an infant. It was like she was on another time zone. She would wake to eat around two or three in the morning, and then she'd be up for three hours. I would carry her downstairs with her happily squealing and bouncing, and tried not to let gravity and exhaustion pull me to the ground right there in the hallway.

I would put on old Kurosawa films. Like most infants, she loved black-and-white patterns and would stare at the screen. I would lie down beside her and we would watch the samurai on their eternal quest for honor. Krista expressed some concern about age appropriateness, but I told her that I would need someone to watch samurai films with me when I was old, and this seemed like the best strategy.

We never allowed Zoey or Allie to watch as much television as Myca. People often comment on how parents are easier on later kids or more likely to spoil them. I don't think it's that, exactly. I used to fight Zoey to change out of her clothes into her pajamas at bedtime. We'd practically wrestle getting her out of a pair of sweats and a T-shirt and into a pair of pajamas that was little more than a pair of sweats and a T-shirt, the only difference being that the pajamas had little cartoon bears on them. When Myca wanted to stay in her sweats and T-shirt at bedtime, I didn't care. I just wanted her to get into bed. She went through a phase of sleeping in frilly dresses. I called them nightgowns and felt proud of myself.

There's this temptation to parent based completely on the ambitions or desires of the adult. This is when you see kids being forced into a certain sport because Dad always wished he could excel at it. Kid actors with overbearing stage parents choosing a career for their toddlers. Or, like Steph's dad, by saying, "You should be a lawyer." That's not all bad, of course. But one thing I've learned is that if I'm going to know my children and they're going to know me, there's something to be said for bringing what my kids love and what I love to the same place, making some alterations, and creating something new.

For instance, I badly wanted my kids to love C. S. Lewis. I had burned through Tolkien by the time I was eight years old, and had gone immediately from there to Narnia. I wanted my kids to go through the Wardrobe and meet Aslan and all the wonderful characters of that fantasy series. But my kids hated it. I tried to read it to them at night and they would shout it down. They absolutely did not want another chapter of "that book." I kept telling them, "It gets better, hang in there, you'll love it!"

They didn't.

I could have forced them to keep listening each night. They would have sat through it if I had made them. But instead I asked them what they didn't like about the books.

"Why is it always British kids?" Zoey asked. "Why can't it be kids like us?"

"I don't want a talking lion," Allie said. "I want a talking tiger."

"And I want a talking horse," Zoey said.

I considered this. "You know, in the Narnia book *A Horse and His Boy*——"

They shouted their reply in unison: "No Narnia books!"

So each night I started telling them a new story I made up. They made edits along the way, but it was the story of a young (American) girl named Validus Smith who, along with her best friend, Alex Shields, travels to another world to help save it from a terrible devouring evil called the Blight. There are talking horses and tigers (and armadillos, sheep, and rabbits). There are, for that matter, talking rocks. Monsters, evil substitute teachers, a magic sword, and the chance to save the world. We used to say, "Validus Smith has three goals: stay alive, save the world, and finish her homework."

My kids loved it. They demanded the story again when it was done. It wasn't Narnia, but it was something better in its way: our own shared world. My kids and I were the only ones who knew about the Passage of the Winds, or who understood the secret of the Sword of Six Worlds. We were the only ones who knew what happened when Alex met the fearsome rock creature who he eventually came to call "Pookie."

The next year I took our story and finally wrote them the book they had been asking about: a fantasy novel called *The Sword of Six Worlds*. It even got published, giving them a chance to share it with their friends.

It became a sort of tradition for us. Most years, at Christmas, I give them a new novel. As they grow older, the types of stories change. A couple of years ago it was a superhero novel called *Capeville*. They loved the heroes in it: the Black Vulture, Jupiter Girl, Lightning Cat, the Gecko, and Pronto—all of them teens fighting against injustice because the adults just can't seem to get it together.

We bring other people into the circle sometimes. When I gave Zoey and Allie *Capeville*, they loved it so much that they wanted to share it with their friends. I had printed only a few vanity copies, so they made a waiting list at school so everyone knew who was next in line to read it. Now their friends know all our superheroes. I had my friend M. S. Corley read it. He's a professional artist and drew pictures of the heroes for us, and even drew a cover for the book. We all obsess over these characters, talk about them, have fun discussing where their stories might go next.

When my friend Tristan recently had a costume party with the theme "obscure superheroes," I went dressed as the Black Vulture, one of the superheroes I had created. I felt slightly geeky (okay, more than slightly) in my black boots and pants, my cape and mask, with the red logo of the Black Vulture on my chest. Allie went as Jupiter Girl. Krista said she would go as the Black Vulture's girlfriend, but as the kids and

Matt takes
Zoey and Allie
for a bike ride
in China (2003).

Allie, Matt, and Zoey
are coerced into singing
"Edelweiss" to several
hundred of Matt's
coworkers (Summer
2007, Beaver Creek
Meadows, Colorado).

On vacation with the
whole family in Krabi,
Thailand, in January
2008. From left to right:
Pete and Maggie (Matt's
parents), Matt, Krista,
Janet and Terry (Krista's
parents), and Zoey and
Allie in the front.

Matt, Myca, Krista, Allie, and Zoey at Panama City Beach, Florida, where Matt often speaks to student groups over spring break (2011).

LEFT: Myca has been riding her scooter in the house since she could stand. As you can see, she also dresses herself in a unique and creative style.

RIGHT: A picture of Steph's note on the sky lantern Matt found in his driveway (November 2014).

The family gathering at Thanksgiving (November 2014). Left to right: Kevin (Krista's brother), Terry, Janet, Matt, Pete, Myca, Maggie, Allie, Aunt Diane (front), Shimmra (in the hat), Zoey, Jonas, and Grandma Traylor.

The mandala made by Anuradha Chandran Menon in honor of her "Acha" after his passing. It took her six days to complete it.

"Princess Kitty" takes out the Black Vulture with a hammer she borrowed from a certain well-known superhero.

ABOVE: Matt and Steph on the first day they met, in Salt Lake City (2015).

RIGHT: Steph's dad, Roberto Aragon, in New Mexico. He always promised her he would take her to see the hot air balloons launch one day . . . one of the reasons she sent a sky lantern in his honor.

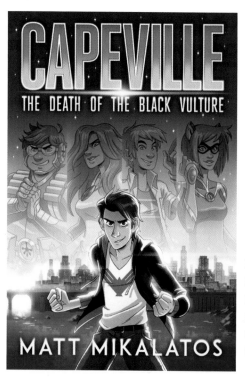

Matt writes novels for his kids for Christmas. Here's the cover to their super hero novel *Capeville*, done by M. S. Corley.

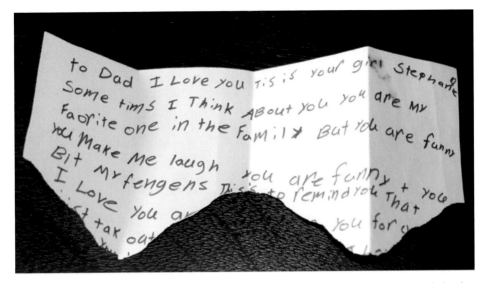

to Dad I Love you Tis is your girl Stephant
Some tims I Think ABout you you are my
Faorite one in the Family * But you are funny
you Make me laugh you are funny + you
Bit my fengens Tis is to remind you That
I Love you a   you for a
... tak out

The note Steph wrote her dad when she was young. He carried it in his wallet until the day he died.

ABOVE: Steph and her dad (center) at a family wedding.

RIGHT: Allie as lead Rose in the rose dance from *Twelve Dancing Princesses* at Northwest Classical Ballet.

Matt and Zoey on her fourteenth birthday. She chose to go to Multnomah Falls for breakfast!

LEFT: Matt and Myca posing with a sky lantern before launch.

RIGHT: Getting ready to let a lantern go. Zoey is in the background, and Myca and Matt in the foreground.

LEFT: Matt McComas and his daughter, Jenna, lighting a sky lantern.

ABOVE: Amy and John Rozzelle, holding Shasta's sky lantern while it fills with hot air.

Getting ready to send
up a lantern of thanks.

Krista and Matt, sending up a lantern on behalf of Steph, with a note for her nephew.

The entire party for our sky lantern launch. Shannon is in the back row, in the gray sweatshirt. Shasta is on the far right in the front row, in the black jacket.

A sky lantern lifting up over the trees at our sky lantern release party (May 2015).

I explained to her, the Black Vulture doesn't have a girlfriend, so she had to go as Rainbow Girl. Myca wore a pink dress and a shiny cat mask and went as Princess Kitty, who had not yet made an appearance in the world of Capeville. Zoey chose a character from the "real" comics called Night Girl.

Maybe it's just me, but I like this life better. Finding common ground between what I love and what the kids love. Finding things out there we can all enjoy. Helping them to understand that their passions, enjoyment, preferences, thoughts, ideas, and opinions are just as important and valid as mine.

That's why I go to ballet recitals several times a year, because Allie loves ballet with a deep passion. That's why Zoey and Krista have carved out so much time to play tennis together. It's why we stand in the rain and watch Myca contentedly running back and forth on a sodden field, completely happy never to put a foot on the soccer ball.

The kids haven't come into my world; we've made new worlds together. I learn from them as often as they learn from me. And a few weeks ago I got a surprise e-mail: it was Zoey's first novel, *Grace's Letters*.

She had written me a book.

19

Letters

"YOU SHOULD WRITE EACH OF YOUR GIRLS A LETTER," Steph had said at our last lunch together. She said it in a way that let me know that it wasn't just a good idea, it was a necessary idea.

It had crossed my mind more than once over the years to write the children letters, but it fell to the bottom of my list of things to be done. It always seemed like there would be more time. But Steph's dad had passed just weeks short of his fifty-seventh birthday. My grandfather passed away when my dad was still a teenager. The human life span is too short. We're like flowers: beautiful, but we fade so quickly.

I had seen how Steph clung to her last letter from her dad, which she kept in her treasure box of remembrances. Letters are, in a sense, a way to freeze time. Steph's dad, Roberto, certainly seemed to think so. He had carried that letter from his little girl until his own grandchildren were older than Steph had been when she wrote it. It was emotional archaeology, a way to remember *This is how we felt once, years ago.*

There is power in this sort of frozen memory. It's like a photograph, only it captures our thoughts instead of our images. Maybe imperfectly, maybe unreliably, but still it's an attempt at communication from the writer to the receiver. Done right, these letters could be a sort of continual communication through the years. You are loved. You might not feel it now. You might have your doubts. But at the very least you must say that you *were* loved once.

Steph was right. Writing her a letter—that momentary act of kindness for a stranger—was life changing. It transformed both of our lives in different ways, all positive. As much as I had come to appreciate Steph, my kids are far more important. Why shouldn't they get a letter from their dad, too? Not some vague letter about my love for them, but a heartfelt, honest, detailed letter.

Which immediately raised this question: how do you explain to a child how amazing they are, and how loved?

I remember when Zoey was born. I talked to her in the womb, feeling her kick a hundred times. I joked that she must be building something in there, she was so busy all the time. Our doctors were named Dr. Neighbor and Dr. Jokey, and they handed her to us in a pink blanket that said "Welcome to the NEIGHBORhood."

A hundred thousand parents have tried to explain that feeling of your child being placed in your arms for the first time. Some might say it's like falling in love. Only worse, only better, only stronger. It's the sudden awareness that you would do anything for this human being, to protect them, keep them safe, provide and help them grow into the beautiful creature he or she has the potential to be. The first time each one of my girls nestled into my arms, I felt exactly that same way.

A letter to my daughters had to be one that assured them that my love wouldn't change in the years to come, no matter what I might say, no matter what choices they made or how the world around us changed. The letter should be both timeless and a time capsule.

In many ways this book is about letters. Steph's note to her father on the sky lantern. My letter to her. The notes we passed back and forth as we got to know each other. The last letter her father sent, and the one she sent him as a child. The letters I would write my own kids. The letters that people from all over the world had sent in response to my letter to Steph.

To attempt to explain to my kids that I love them and feel proud to be their father is by necessity an exercise in short-hand. Just reflecting back on my day, I can think of examples.

This morning Zoey wore a pink shirt to school. She's in eighth grade, and two days ago one of the other students committed suicide. Before we rolled out the door, she noticed on social media that some of the kids were going to wear pink for suicide prevention, so she went to change. I asked her if she knew the kid and she told me no, but some of her friends did. She shared what a terrible thing it was and how she had seen another student crying the day before and walked up to her and just hugged her without saying a word. That was this morning. I couldn't love her more or be more proud of her than in that moment.

Today Allie came bouncing down the steps dressed like someone from a Harry Potter movie. She asked me to tie her Hogwarts tie. It was "*Harry Potter* vs. *Hunger Games*" for Spirit Week at school, and she was ready to go. She made ridiculous jokes all morning. She teased me when I couldn't remember the name of the youngest redheaded daughter in the Weasley family. Two miles from the school, she realized it was actually "Presidents vs. Aliens" Day, and she laughed about it. We made jokes about presidents the rest of the way, and when she got out of the car she said, "See you tomorrow," even though I would see her in seven hours, just because she thought that was funny. That was this morning. And I couldn't love her more or be more proud of her.

This afternoon, after crowing like a rooster while riding her scooter home, Myca demanded some applesauce. While she ate it she gave me this health advice: "Applesauce is good for you because it is full of oranges." When I went to lie on our hammock, she came and curled up next to me. When I hugged one of the other kids, she burst into tears and said I hadn't hugged her lately. Tonight, before she went to church, she cut out paper and drew tiny Crayola pictures of her with one of the youth workers and wrote notes about all the things she liked about her. That was today. I couldn't love her more or be more proud of her.

That's one day. How I am supposed to boil down fourteen years of days with Zoey to explain my love for her? Twelve years for Allie? Five for Myca? These letters, no matter how amazing, will be a distillation, an approximation, an attempt at explaining to them what I feel and think about them, and how amazing they are. They'll have to take my word for it when I say, "It's much more than this, my darlings. There are not sufficient words to explain this to you. You'll have to take it on faith that when I say I love you it's more than you know. When I say I am proud of you, it's without qualifiers. When I say I want you to have a good life, it's with a bone-aching depth of desire that is not matched by any other want in my life."

So, where to start? It's tempting to start with "The first time I held you in my arms, everything changed." Because that's the truth, and it's this moment as a parent that you can't put into words: how the world goes dim and loses its color when your child is cradled in your arms; how they become your bright, sharp center and change your purpose.

I could try to explain that even before knowing if they would be kind or cruel, or if they would be intelligent or not, and before knowing if they would be serious or hilarious, I already loved them. Or that when their only accomplishment was drawing in one shaky breath and letting out a tiny baby cry, I was proud of them. Love and acceptance came before any decision they made. Pride came before any action on their part, before any revelation of their character or personality.

But, in the end, they won't understand that—not in the way I would want them to. So I am going to try something different: I am going to write them love letters in their own language, in the language of their passions.

If they don't understand, I will tell them again, with different words, until they do.

20

Zoey

Dear Zoey,

Love is a story.

   Watching your passion for books from the time you were able to flip a page is one of the great joys of my life. I remember you lying on the floor as a toddler in the doorway to your room, not wanting to go to bed and carefully studying a pile of books, right where you could look down the hallway to see me and your mom.

Every day I see you writing in one of your notebooks, filling them with your novels. I can't believe that you, already at the age of fourteen, have written two novels. You're amazing. I can't wait to see what stories you will bring to us in the years to come.

My love for you is like the love you have for the hero in a book you've read over and over. She's brave, and strong, and kind to those in need, and when she makes mistakes she owns up to them and becomes a better person. Those things are true about you, too. Just like you want to open that book and go through her story again, my attention keeps turning back to you. I want to know your story. I want to cheer when you defeat the villains. I want to know what will happen next.

I am amazed by your certainty of yourself. You have a knowledge of what you want, what you like, and don't allow other people to sway your opinion on those things. Of course this is maddening to people who want to change your behavior (I would like, for instance, to figure out how to get you to eat vegetables!), but it's beautiful that you know who you are and refuse to compromise that for the sake of other people's desires.

I am proud of how clever you are. You work out solutions to difficult problems and quickly solve mysteries.

Your love of science and your voracious desire to learn animate your features—you overflow with life when you're learning. While navigating the towers of books in your room is both dangerous and terrifying, the way you devour those books is inspiring and beautiful. When you said you were going to read every book of fiction in your middle school library before you graduated, I was skeptical. I know not to doubt you now!

I enjoy it when you seek after the things you are passionate about: tennis, science and math, writing, reading, horses, dolphins. Even sharks, which you know are not my favorite animals. I love watching you give Myca piggyback rides. I am so happy when you and Allie are off doing activities together. Everyone is thankful when you make waffles in the mornings, or when you decide to bake cookies. Your ridiculous jokes and proverbs and riddles make me laugh. (Always remember, "The early bird gets the worm, but the second mouse gets the cheese.")

You are a beautiful, wonderful young woman. I do not love you because of the things you have done, good or bad. I love you because you are my daughter. Nothing you can do will ever change that. My love for you is bigger than any choices you might make in the years to come.

You are a gifted and talented young woman. I am

amazed by your intellect and passion. I am not proud of you because of your accomplishments; you have already accomplished enough for me to be proud of you for the rest of your life. No matter what comes, know that I am proud of you and so glad to be your father.

You deserve the best, and in the years to come I hope you will not settle for something less. Whether it's by your friends, by your spouse if you should choose to marry, or in your vocation, you deserve to be treated with respect, honor, equality, and dignity.

Zoey, love is a story, and here is ours: Once upon a time there was a man who married and had a daughter. Her name was Zoey, which means life, *because she was the first life he had helped to make. And though there were hard times, and though there were misunderstandings, her father treasured her in all the years to come. And they lived happily ever after.*

Love always,

Dad

21

Allie

Dear Allie,

Love is a dance.

    I remember you taking your first ballet class at the community center, and how you would always plan new jokes for Miss Patty, and how she would pretend to laugh even when they weren't funny, and how delighted you were that you had made her smile.

Your passion for and dedication to ballet are amazing. Watching you, five days a week, how you practice and work hard and keep going to try to get a tiny bit better, to jump higher, to keep your legs straighter, to make your form slightly better, to hold your hands correctly, is inspiring. The choreography you do, and your focus on making the world a better place even in the topics you address in your dances, is amazing.

My love for you is like the love you have for dancing. I want to be an expert in knowing you. I want to spend my extra moments at the end of the day thinking about you and getting to know you better. And, like a young ballerina dedicated to her craft, real love gets better and stronger, more accomplished, more dedicated, more proficient, more powerful.

I am not surprised that you love ballet. It's more than dancing: it is an art that requires not just devotion and discipline but an aspiration to be someone extraordinary. It requires a desire to be exceptional, to be marvelous. It is an art that recognizes the beauty not only in the dancer but in the people around the dancer, that shows respect to your fellow dancers, to the musicians, the teacher, and the audience. It is about kindness, and generosity, art, beauty, and creativity.

These are all things I see and love in you.

Your dedication and discipline are a wonder to me. I

can't believe that you have skipped friends' birthday parties to go to rehearsal, that you have made sacrifices for your art at your age. I enjoy watching how you have grown stronger, more dedicated, more able to do spectacular things on the stage because of your commitment.

At the same time, you're smart and a hard worker at school. You have a natural way of drawing people together and building not just friendships but communities of people who all enjoy each other. Your kindness to children and to those with less social standing than you always warms my heart.

The level of your ridiculous humor doesn't come across in your dances, but I suppose one day it might. As you know, I enjoy your crazy songs and the weird dances you invent with your friends, and your consistent desire to correct my Spanish even when I say Hasta banana to you every single night. Don't worry, I'm sure one day I'll learn to say Hasta bañana like you want me to.

As you grow older I hope you'll remember that most anything worth doing requires the same focus, attention, and attributes that you show in your dancing: commitment, discipline, passion, creativity, generosity to others, awareness of those around you. I know you will find a way to make your entire life an exceptional dance.

You are a beautiful, wonderful young woman. I do not

love you because of the things you have done, good or bad. I love you because you are my daughter. Nothing you can do will ever change that. My love for you is bigger than any choices you might make in the years to come.

You are a gifted and talented young woman. I am amazed by your dedication and creativity. I am not proud of you because of your accomplishments: you have already accomplished enough for me to be proud of you for the rest of your life. No matter what comes, know that I am proud of you and so glad to be your father.

Like Clara in The Nutcracker, *you deserve the greatest, most wonderful life, and in the years to come I hope you will not settle for something less. Whether it's by your friends, by your spouse if you should choose to marry, or in your vocation, you deserve to be treated with respect, honor, equality, and dignity.*

Allie, love is like a dance. From the moment you entered the stage, I fell in love with this dance and with you. And though there may come moments when the dance is difficult, or the music becomes muddied, or the steps are not quite in rhythm, this is a dance that I treasure, and I know that will not change in the years to come.

Love always,

Dad

22

Myca

Dear Myca,

Love is a hummingbird.

   Do you know that feeling when you are running with your
friends, playing soccer, and the ball goes by you and all your
friends are running in the same direction and you feel safe
and surrounded by your friends, and a big smile comes on
your face and you start to laugh as you run, and then you
crow at the top of your lungs? That is how I feel about you.

Remember when Mom was teaching you how to read, and how every night you were reading another story in that very long book? And do you remember how you felt when you read the last story in that book, how proud you were and how you danced around the room and cheered and then for several days you kept picking up the book and reading a few pages because you knew you could? That's how I feel about you.

You know how at night, when you're getting ready for bed, how you absolutely must have a certain stuffed animal? Right now it is your hummingbird. She's small and green with a white chest and a red throat, and you take that bird with you everywhere.

You are like that hummingbird!

You are unique and beautiful. You move from place to place with astonishing speed, you have a very strange and limited diet, and when you are still you are often singing! I love the kind way you interact with the people around you. I remember when you were very small and one of your sisters was crying and you toddled over to her and gave her a hug and rubbed her back and said, "It's okay, it's okay." Your drawings and stories are wonderful, and you have a special way of making all the people around you have fun.

You're great at math and seem to keep a map of the

world in your head. You notice things no else seems to see.
When you were born, we let your sisters choose a middle
name for you and they chose Anne, which means favor or
grace. Grace means a gift that is given to someone even
if they don't deserve something so wonderful, and that is
what you are to all of us: an amazing, wonderful gift, and
much more than we deserve.

You are a beautiful, wonderful young woman. I do not
love you because of the things you have done, good or bad.
I love you because you are my daughter. Nothing you can
do will ever change that. My love for you is bigger than any
choices you might make in the years to come.

You are a kind and creative young woman. I am amazed
by your unique way of looking at the world and your love
for the people around you. I am not proud of you because
of your accomplishments: you have already accomplished
enough for me to be proud of you for the rest of your life.
No matter what comes, know that I am proud of you and so
glad to be your father.

Just like a hummingbird gets a special kind of feeder
with special food, or drinks from the sweetest flowers, you
deserve to be treated as the unique, wonderful, special
young woman you are, and in the years to come I hope
you will not settle for something less. Whether it's by your

friends, by your spouse if you should choose to marry, or in your vocation, you deserve to be treated with respect, honor, equality, and dignity.

Myca, love is a hummingbird. Beautiful, quick, shining, and free. If you're ready for it, if you're paying attention, it hovers near you. And if you look closely, you'll see it is never far away, and it always returns. You'll see it outside the window, in the garden, near the flowers. And though there may be seasons when it seems absent or you may feel you're not seeing it often, you can know it's always nearby. If you are still, and if you listen carefully, you may hear it singing in the maple tree outside your bedroom.

I love you, and my love will always find you, my dear child. Love has wings that move faster than you can see.

Love always,

Dad

23

Invisible

A FEW DAYS BEFORE THANKSGIVING, I HAD STOPPED TO pick up some trash in my front yard. A note caught my eye and touched my heart. It took me a little over an hour to write a letter to a woman I barely knew. That small act of kindness—tiny, inconsequential—had enormous healing power for people all over the world. Certainly for my new friend, Steph. Now it had even begun to work in my own family, as I tried to better express my love for my own kids.

It had not required much effort, honestly: a moment's attention to the world around me, a few moments to consider that world from the point of view of another person, to see her hurting and reach out. I was surprised by how this small kindness had brought healing to other people and to myself—how it had changed the world around me. So I began an experiment. A minor, tiny, inconsequential experiment. What if I tried to do some small act of kindness like that once a week? Something small that wouldn't take me more than an hour or so. Something I could fit into my life without much trouble.

My little acts tended to take less time than I thought—even less than an hour. Putting someone else's dishes in the dishwasher (sometimes multiple someones). Calling a friend who had a hard day, just because their name came to mind. Helping a stranger find something they dropped at the movie theater. Running over to let my neighbor know their garage door was still open. Little things that may not have changed the world or the people around me but seemed to be changing me.

Changing me how?

In one specific way: it was helping me to see others—their world, their needs, their desires—more than my own, because I was watching the people around me, asking if there was a small, kind action I could take. Not all the time. Not every moment. In fact, I found that I slipped easily into thinking about myself and, instead of acting in kindness, I'd get wrapped up in the inconvenience others were causing me. When I'm focused on myself, it's hard to get a sense of scale. My inconvenience is larger and more important than someone else's tragedy.

Here's my biggest example from the last several months.

I was speaking at a conference in Florida, at Panama City Beach. It was spring break, and the streets were clogged with college students. They drove up and down Front Street, all of them in swim trunks and bikinis, music blaring, windows down, looking for love. Some of them were drunk, or high, or both. Many had rented tiny unsafe deathtrap motor scooters, which they used to thread through traffic, howling, the plastic beads around their necks flying back in the wind, flip-flops on the footrests, no helmets on at all, and rarely any shirts.

I was running late for my talk that night. It was a talk about seeing the invisible people around you, how important they are, how necessary it is that we see and care for other human beings, how beautiful and essential they are, how loved by God and thus how we, too, should love them. Ordinarily I would have walked across a sky bridge from my hotel room to the conference center, but because I was late I decided to drive the short distance.

I got to my rental car and drove off the property onto the public road. But the intersection was completely blocked. Police cars everywhere. In the middle of the intersection there was the burnt-out shell of a van and the crushed remnants of two motor scooters. My first thought was annoyance that I was going to be late. Going to repark my car would take too long, so I parked it there on the side of the road and decided to make a run for the conference center on foot. I would come back for the car later.

As I got closer to the intersection, I saw clumps of college kids standing at the four corners. Some were crying. Some were praying. Some were laughing and making jokes.

I asked one of them what had happened.

"A van ran a red light and drove over a scooter. It caught on fire. They took three people away in ambulances and arrested the van driver. Somebody died, man."

A college student dead, and here I was, worried about being five minutes late.

On the far side of the intersection a kid sat on the curb, head in his hands, barefoot and alone. The cops, the other college kids—everyone—seemed to be giving him space.

"What's that guy's story?" I asked.

"He was in the van."

I was worried about my talk, and there was a kid on the side of the road who had just been in a car that literally ran over another human being. I had been inconvenienced. His life had been shaken. I felt as if someone had sat down hard on my chest.

I crossed the intersection, being careful to stay clear of the wreckage of the van and the scooters. I sat down beside the kid on the sidewalk, both of us washed in the blue and red lights from the nearby police car. He wore a loose sleeveless shirt, baggy shorts, and a backward baseball cap.

"You okay?" I asked.

"Yeah. I just . . . We just came down here to have fun. My friend was driving and I don't know what he was doing. I was yelling at him to stop, stop, stop, stop! But he didn't even hit the brakes; he just . . . he just rode straight over them. Then the van was on fire and I jumped out and they took him to jail. I guess he killed that guy. That's not why we came here, though. We just wanted to have some fun."

He went on like that, his stories going in circles. I talked to him for a while and tried to help him calm down, and offered help if he needed it. His friend was in jail and he didn't know the kids on the scooters, but he was thinking about going down to the hospital to see how they were doing. (A miraculous aside: the kid who had gone under the van hadn't died. They revived him in the ambulance and he lived.) His cell phone had been in the van. He didn't have a way to get back to his hotel.

I stayed with him until the cops released him, and I gave him a ride. We talked about his hometown, his family. We talked about spiritual things. He looped back to the accident more than once. I wrote my number on a scrap of paper and he shoved it deep into the pocket of his shorts.

"Thanks, man," he said. "I mean it. You giving me a ride . . . that's amazing. Thank you."

I never saw him again.

Never heard from him.

Did that little act of kindness change his life? I don't know. But it changed mine. It reminded me that I needed to stop seeing myself as the most important person on any given day. I needed to learn to see through myself, to let me be invisible so that other people could come into focus. Sure, that could be taken to an unhealthy extreme, but I was a long way from that.

I was only twenty minutes late to my meeting. I had spent fifteen minutes with that college kid. That's it. Fifteen minutes of my day, set aside for a small kindness, and I think it was better spent than any other fifteen minutes of that week.

I'm not a police officer—I don't see accidents every day. I'm not a chaplain or a doctor—I don't see life-and-death situations every week.

Seems like most days my greatest chance at being kind is to do something small.

A few weeks ago I sat in my bed writing this book. Myca crawled up beside me and curled alongside my leg.

"Why is my name on there?" she asked.

"I'm writing a book."

"Are you writing about me?"

"Yes."

She gave me a skeptical sideways look. "You will make this into a book?"

"Yes."

She thought about this. "Can I choose the cover?"

"No. The publisher does that."

"Read it to me."

So I read to her from chapter six, the section where I talked about our morning rituals and how each morning Myca sat at the kitchen counter and chose the color of bowl she would like, and I poured her some cereal. She asked me to count the number of times her name appeared in the book, and I did that, too.

She said, "Change that story to say 'she chooses the color

of the plate' that she will use for breakfast and then say 'she eats waffles every day.' "

"But you don't eat waffles every day," I said. "You're not eating waffles today, either."

She glared at me. "Just change it."

I didn't change it.

Instead, I woke early the next morning. A chorus of sparrows greeted the new sun in the plum tree outside my bedroom window, but the rest of the house lay cool and silent.

I woke her with the smell of waffles, fresh and hot from the iron.

24

Constellations

I THOUGHT FLYING SKY LANTERNS WOULD BE FUN. I didn't realize how much work it would be. It didn't matter, because I wanted to experience it. I wanted to take my family and friends out to a wide space and release the lanterns, then watch them rise into the blue light of early evening.

I did some research and found biodegradable, fire-resistant lanterns.

I called the fire department to make sure it was legal to fly them and under what conditions.

I bought an extinguisher.

But we still needed a place to launch the lanterns.

We live too close to an airport and our neighbors to fly them at our house. Most parks close at dusk. I thought about sneaking onto the property of a local school, but I kept having visions of the police arresting us for trespassing. You can't easily hide flying, glowing lanterns.

Krista suggested I call some old family friends, Mark and Cheryl. They have a pasture for their horses. There aren't many houses nearby, and it's more than five miles from the airport. I asked Mark if we could come out the next evening to launch lanterns, and he said that would be fine.

I sent a note to a few people, asking if they could come, and the next night our house filled up with friends, all ready to give it a try. Most of them had heard about Steph and wanted to be part of this.

The first to arrive, all of them with children in tow, were Joe and Shannon Emery, followed by Matt and Jody Mc-Comas. I got out the lanterns and some markers and we started decorating and writing messages on them.

"What should we write?" Shannon asked.

"Whatever you want," I said. "Some people write notes to loved ones, or prayers, or things like that. But I don't think we all need to write notes to dead people. We can write whatever we want. I did think it would be nice to do one lantern that was just prayers for Shasta. Do you think that would be okay?"

Over a year earlier, our friend Shasta Kramer started treatment for stage two breast cancer. She had gone to college with Krista and joined the same nonprofit we did at the same time. We went through training together for the organization. Over the years she has become part of our family. The kids think of her as their aunt. She's been to countless holiday celebrations at our house and our parents' houses. She's one of my best friends.

During treatment, a lot of us pitched in, but the two families most involved were ours and Shannon and Joe's. Shannon and Shasta are best friends, too. They lived together in Italy for a year, once upon a time. Between me and Shannon, one of us had been to nearly every one of Shasta's doctor appointments.

Shasta is a vibrant person, full of life, the one most likely to start a spontaneous dance party, the one the kids all love to see walk in the door, the one who starts the water fight at the Fourth of July picnic. As the chemotherapy killed the cancer, the vibrant, lively Shasta we all knew slowly lost her energy and became so weak that she could barely get out of bed some days. Her hair fell out, including her eyelashes. She needed help doing the dishes, making meals, changing her sheets.

We were so relieved after chemo to hear that her cancer had responded well. Once the surgeries and radiation were done, she started to bounce back and had been slowly becoming her old self again. Her hair was back, and her energy had largely returned.

Then, a few months later, she found another lump.

A series of scans and tests and biopsies showed that her cancer had returned and, worse, it had spread. The cancer was now stage four, in both breasts and in her lungs now, too. There would be more treatments, more doctor appointments, and more hard times to come.

I asked Shannon, "Do you think Shasta would be okay with us doing a lantern full of prayers for her?"

Shannon said, "I think it would be a good thing."

"It might make her cry."

"It's okay if she cries." I understood what she meant. It's a different thing to cry because your friends love you than to cry because of an illness. Shannon, Shasta, and I had all cried in plenty of hospital rooms in the last couple of months. This was probably true of nearly everyone at the party . . . Shasta is well loved.

Shannon was the first to write on Shasta's lantern, followed by Joe. Krista took pictures of the notes people wrote, a sweet gesture to make sure that Shasta was able to see each prayer and hold on to them after the lantern was gone.

Meanwhile, more people arrived at the house. Katie and Lucas Quarles and their son, Boaz. Angie and Adam Lausche and their kids. Shasta showed up as well. A few more friends texted to say they would meet us at Mark's house.

Krista ran to get Allie at ballet, and I started the process of getting everyone out of the house. I hunted for Myca and found her with Joe and Shannon's daughter, Sienna, the two of them careening around the house like pinballs. I waved Myca over, her sneakers in my hands.

"Myca, time to put on your shoes."

She did a strange little dance, probably showing off for Sienna, and said, "Where are my sockie-wockies?"

"They're in your shoesie-woosies," I said, handing them over.

Sienna cocked her head and looked up at me, a half-delighted, half-serious look on her face, and said, "You are funny." It's nice that kids enjoy something as simple as call-and-response rhyming.

The sun was still up when we got to Mark's. Nicole Lewis, Tristan Boyce, and John and Amy Rozzelle were all waiting for us when our vehicles pulled into the long driveway. The kids bounced from the cars, running to see the horses, which had ambled up to the pasture fence, leaning across to get their noses rubbed.

Mark brought carrots for the kids to feed the horses, and I pulled the sky lanterns out and put them on the hood of my car so people could finish decorating them. As dusk settled around us, we gathered along the northern edge of the pasture. Matt and his daughter Jenna agreed to send up their lantern first. Matt held it up. The lanterns were larger than I expected when the paper was unfolded. The square fuel cell was held in by string.

I lit the square and Matt and I held the lantern, waiting for the flame to heat the air that would lift the lantern. Jenna took my place holding the lantern and we waited for a moment, trying to keep it from folding in toward the flame. A slight breeze was blowing.

When we released the lantern, it shot up, a warm glow that slid into the breeze and rose above our heads, escaping to the southeast, over the pasture, clearing the trees. We craned our necks to watch it go. We moved to follow it better, to see the lantern bob in the wind, dwindling away to the size of a soccer ball, a grapefruit, a baseball, a quarter, a star.

We handed out the other lanterns. Night had arrived. I dropped the lighter once and couldn't see it on the dark ground. We could only see one another in silhouette until a lantern flared to life. The warm glow washed over us as we held the lanterns, waiting for them to be ready, waiting for them to rise. As they ascended, we would return to shadow, but we weren't looking at one another, we were tracking those glowing paper lanterns floating skyward. We shouted and laughed. We pointed and said, "That one's yours!" We gasped when they were carried by the wind. We cheered when they cleared the trees.

The children circled us like planets around newly lit stars. The whole evening began to feel like a ritual in the best sense of the word. It felt like a holiday: like this action was full of meaning—that it was somehow a tradition, although few of us had done it before. I had expected it to be fun, but I hadn't expected this.

I couldn't put a name to the feeling—not at first—but I could hear the frogs singing in the pasture and the sound of the horses walking over, curious. I could hear children laughing and crying, thrilled to be awake in the dark night, exhausted, exhilarated. I could hear my friends and family— ten conversations happening at once as we spread out, lit lanterns, talked about life, enjoyed one another, took pictures, sent our deepest thoughts, prayers, and feelings toward the heavens.

The lanterns rose. One at first, and then several, soaring like a flock of strange but gentle birds. I could almost believe that they would go higher—up beyond sight—rising to heaven and taking our words and wishes and hopes somewhere far from there to someone who has answers to our wants, our needs, our grief.

John and Amy lit Shasta's lantern, and the flame filled it with golden light. The words on the paper skin were suffused with radiance that seemed to come not from the flame but from the words themselves, and as the lantern rose, I couldn't help but stop to look at the people gathered there in that field. They were watching the lantern climb higher, all of them holding their collective breath, willing the lantern not to burn or collapse in the wind. Willing it to leave us, to find answers somewhere and somehow bring them back to us. Watching my family and friends, their black shadows against the deepening blue of the sky, I knew the name for this feeling.

This night felt holy. Releasing these lanterns felt sacred.

"That's your lantern," I said. It had left the pasture and was drifting above the trees. I grabbed Shasta's arm and pointed again. "There it is. Right there, that's yours."

Another lantern rose into the sky. Every time, it caught our attention. Everyone stopped to see. Would this one make it? Each lantern was a victory, a reminder that we could overcome gravity, if only for a moment. I helped send another lantern up. A few minutes later I turned to see Shasta standing nearby, staring up into the clear sky. Shannon stood beside her.

"Is that my lantern?" Shasta asked.

Shannon, her best friend, leaned close and looked up to where Shasta pointed. "I think that's a star."

Maybe it was a star.

Maybe it was her lantern.

Maybe her lantern had become a star, a beacon shining our prayers into the night sky.

We were—all of us—watching the lanterns, watching the stars. My heart lifted up like a lantern, full of warmth and light. Full, for the first time in many months, with hope.

25

Miracles

WE LINGERED AT OUR CARS, SAYING OUR GOOD-BYES, HUG-
ging one another, promising to write or call or text and get
together soon. I felt intensely grateful for each person there
who had made the time at the last minute to stand in a field
and send shining lanterns into the heavens.

It was three hours past bedtime for Myca, but she was full
of buoyant, happy pleasantries all the way home. She curled
up in bed with a warm, satisfied smile. I prayed for her—for

good dreams and deep sleep. She frowned when I finished. "You forgot to say thank you for a good day that had sky lanterns," she said. "Do it over." So I prayed again, this time with thankfulness clearly stated, and she drifted off in a few minutes, much like a lantern herself, her small light gliding over dreamscapes of trees and valleys, tiny houses lit below, the river glinting in moonlight.

Shasta texted me that she had driven the back roads of our town, looking for spent lanterns. She wanted to see where they would land, but found nothing. She said it had been a wonderful night. I told her it had felt holy to me. Nicole wrote and said the same thing: fun night, holy night. Other friends wrote to thank us for inviting them. The kids raved about it. Everyone enjoyed themselves.

I told Steph it had gone well, that it had been fun and beautiful. She had joked with me about flying out to come watch, and I wish that had been a possibility. I had told her I would write on a lantern for her, and she sent me a message for her nephew who passed away the previous year. His tombstone was next to her father's.

Her note said, "To my angel in the sky: I love you. I think of you every day. Watch over us . . . #DEA #Daniel Aragon53 #nephew Always Love, Aunt Steph." It was simple and sweet: an address of sorts, her feelings for him, a request for protection, his initials, his name and football jersey number, their relationship, and of course a reminder that death cannot sever love. "Thanks for sending one for me," she said. "I wonder if they use hashtags in heaven. Maybe I will get another miracle."

Another miracle.

Watching those lanterns race across the pasture above our heads and into the night, I could see it was more than a strange coincidence that Steph's lantern had made its way to me. We had no idea where ours had gone, no way to find them or bring them back. Yet somehow Steph's had found me, had brought us together, making its way to me so that we could become friends, so that she could feel her father's presence for one more moment, so our lives could be enriched with new friendships. So that I could stand, surrounded by people I dearly loved, and send my own lantern—our lanterns—to make more miracles.

To me, the miracle wasn't so much that Steph's lantern had found me; it was that we had found each other. Friends are the miracle. Finding a new friend increases the room in our hearts for love. It's a lesson we've all learned at some point. When my children were born, my heart grew larger. Love is like a fire: it spreads. The tiniest spark of love can grow into a massive fire. And my love for my children caused a response of love in them for me. Children love their parents because their parents loved them first.

The world is full of these miracles. There is beauty on every corner, near us at every moment. When we first walked out to the pasture that day, before the sun had set, Shannon and Joe's toddler, Chiara, raced for the fence and catapulted herself through the beams. Her parents were shouting for her to come back, not to do that, and her dad unlatched the gate and ran after her to grab her. She ran to the north end of the pasture where a spray of yellow wildflowers had sprouted, and she stood in the center of them, looking back at us with a smile of triumphant pleasure. A year from now, she will have grown out of such things, but today it is beautiful and fleeting and precious.

Just in our few hours together there were so many small kindnesses. Mark letting us use his field and teaching the children how to feed the horses. Krista roving around, taking pictures so we could remember it. Tristan videoing the whole affair. Nicole with a kind word and conversation for everyone. Friendships strengthening in our shared experience. All of us watching the children without regard to whether we are their parents, keeping them safe, keeping them close.

When it was time to fly Steph's new lantern, Krista, Zoey, Allie, and Myca came near. We lit it together, washed in its radiance. We let it go too soon, before it was fully warmed up, and it dipped away from us. As it crossed the pasture the sky lantern flew low—too low—and I ran after it, worried it would crash and we would need to stomp out the flames. It began to rise slowly, but it flew faster than I could run. It crossed a dry creek bed. I leapt down into it, discovering it was in fact a mud pit, and my foot sank halfway to my knee.

Now the lantern rocketed upward. I had worried for nothing. I turned to see one of Adam and Angie's kids, her purple hood pulled up over her head as she stood on the edge of the drop. She had followed me, running to see the lantern sail, my sudden sprint her invitation to see where it would go—to chase it—to be near it a moment longer.

"Be careful," I said, my foot making a sucking sound as I pulled it out of the mud. "Don't come any closer, it's muddy." I climbed up beside her on the bank of the creek. "You followed me, huh?"

"Yes," she said in a small and certain voice.

"Can I carry you back to your daddy?"

"Yes." She lifted her arms to me and I scooped her up. We walked back toward the circle of warmth and light, back to the company of our families.

The lanterns rose, some of them with messages of love for departed loved ones. Some with prayers, or scriptures, or small sayings. Some with beautiful patterns, with flowers and trees, with notes of thankfulness or hope. One of the kids had drawn stick "bunnies with no ears." The thing they all had in common was their origin: these messages—these notes and wishes and prayers—had come from us.

I had been surprised, when the moment came, how vulnerable it felt to write an honest message on my lantern. To write my note among my family and friends was not the problem. I try to be honest and vulnerable with them. But who knew how far this lantern might go? Who knew where it might land? Who knew what stranger's hands might pick it up on the other end?

It's a risk to write our true feelings where others can see them. We worry how people will react. By definition, vulnerability means that we could be hurt. We are vulnerable. We are afraid. Of course we are afraid! We are sensitive, fragile creatures, short-lived and wanting love. We are yellow flowers in a pasture, and our vibrant colors fade too quickly. We are flares of light, bright but brief in this engulfing dark. But, oh, so beautiful!

I am lying in bed now. Myca is asleep. Zoey and Allie have wandered through and said their good-nights. Their lights are off and they are safe and at peace, their dreams decorated with edelweiss and lanterns. Krista and I have talked about the night and she has rolled onto her side, breathing softly. All our friends are home now, going through their own evening rituals.

I am lying in bed, but I am still in that pasture. Though my eyes are closed, I can still see.

The lanterns are rising up into the dark like small, temporary stars.

Who knows where they may go? Who might find them? This spark that lights the lantern's fuel could be the spark of some great adventure, more than we imagined, more than we hope.

This lantern might be the beginning of a new friendship—might expand the world's capacity for love.

It may coast past someone mourning a miscarriage and startle them out of their grief.

This lantern may glide by some teenagers, and they, laughing, may run after it, pulling it to earth in a moment of pure joy.

Perhaps this lantern will lighten our hearts, lift them above our everyday concerns.

God only knows what may come of them.

Somewhere in the dark above my house, the warm lights flicker and fade, much faster than we would expect, much sooner than we would hope. The lanterns wink out, their brief lights illuminating the darkness for only a handful of minutes.

But, oh, so beautiful!

And somewhere in the distant darkness, someone else lights a flame.

Acknowledgments

K ARL B ARTH ONCE SAID, "J OY IS THE SIMPLEST FORM OF gratitude." Here are a few people who brought me joy while writing this book:

My wife, Krista, who was the first to say this story should be a book, and the one who made the most adjustments to make room for me to write it. Thank you!

Wes Yoder, who helped shape the idea and gave excellent advice and encouragement along the way (as always!).

ACKNOWLEDGMENTS

Ami McConnell, who convinced me the book was a memoir. Your insights shaped this book more than anyone else's. I am immensely grateful you suggested we do our own lantern party. Thank you.

Katie Sandell, editor extraordinaire. Thank you for your hard work and great editing. Thanks also to the team at Howard Books. There wouldn't be a book without you. I am thankful.

Zoey, Allie, and Myca, thank you for letting me put you in the spotlight once again.

House Morgasteros (JR, Amanda, and Clay), who read drafts and proposals and gave insights and moral support. Especially Amanda. Because she read it first.

Steph Aragón. Thank you for being generous with your story and your friendship. (Steph wanted to add this acknowledgment: "My sons, Nicholas and Darrian, you will always be the most important humans in my life. You taught me everything I know about love and sacrifice. I love you without end.")

Anuradha Chandran Menon. Thank you for sharing your art, poetry, and deep thoughts about your father. (See more of Anu's art at http://tinyurl.com/anumalight.)

M. S. Corley, thanks for your friendship and for bringing Capeville to life! It's amazing to see my characters "live" through your art! (See it at www.mscorley.com.)

Shasta Kramer. Thank you for sharing your story here and in everyday life. You bring peace to those around you. I am praying for your healing. Aloha nui loa from me, our family, and your many friends.

To my parents, Pete and Maggie, and Krista's, Janet and Terry. Thank you for your love, support, and kindness. It's an honor to be in your families. (Thanks also to Kevin, Shimmra, Jonas, Aunt Diane, Grandma Traylor, Dawn, Todd, and Lynn!)

To everyone who came to our sky lantern launch party: Mark and Cheryl Johnson, who let us use their property, and also Joe and Shannon Emery, Lucas and Katie Quarles, Nicole Lewis, Tristan Boyce, John and Amy Rozzelle, Matt and Jody McComas, Adam and Angie Lausche, and of course all the many kids who came along!

To all of you who passed along my letter to Steph, this is your story, too. Thank you for sharing that letter with your friends and loved ones. Joy and peace to you in the years to come.

Enhance Your Book Club

THIS BOOK CLUB DISCUSSION GUIDE HAS BEEN BROKEN into chunks of roughly four chapters per section. Feel free to do them all at once or spread them out over time. On a limited basis, Matt is available to do online chats or group phone calls with book clubs. He really enjoys talking to people about this book and their thoughts and experiences. Feel free to write him at SkyLantern@mikalatos.com to schedule a book chat with your group!

CHAPTERS 1-4

1 Have you ever seen or launched a sky lantern? Describe what that experience was like. Did you enjoy it or not?

2 What was your first thought when you read the note from Steph? What would you have done if you had found the lantern?

3 In chapter 2, Matt shares a deep loss and how a moment of light startled him out of his grief. Has that ever happened to you? If you feel comfortable, share your experience with the group.

4 In chapter 3, a key reason Matt writes the letter to Steph is that he imagines what it would be like for his kids if he were to die. What do you think of that thought process? Is it a healthy exercise or not?

5 In chapter 4, Matt says he realized the lantern was a call for help. Do you think you would have come to the same conclusion? Have you seen or heard someone cry for help in some way before? What did you do? What happened? Do you wish you had done anything differently?

CHAPTERS 5-8

1 In chapter 5, at last, we get to Matt's letter. What were you thinking and feeling as you read it? What specific emotions did it stir in you? Did you think about a specific person in your life when you read it?

2 Matt's basic message falls into three categories: love, be loved, and live a good life. Which of these is hardest for you? Which is easiest? Do you believe that there is someone in the world who loves you and is proud of you?

3 Matt ends his letter with the belief that "love is as strong as death." Discuss this thought and if you agree or disagree. How does Matt's letter support this belief?

4 In chapter 6, Matt talks about "Edelweiss" and how he showed love to his daughters. How do you show love to important people in your life? Do you have certain rituals or traditions? Have these slowly changed over time?

5 Matt ends chapter 6 saying, "We have to send our love out into the world so people will find it." Do you agree or disagree? Why?

6   Are you surprised by the strong response others had to the letter? Why or why not?

7   In chapter 8, Matt talks about thankfulness. Is being thankful easy or hard for you? Do you agree that we always have something to be thankful for, even in difficult times?

CHAPTERS 9-13

1   Chapter 9 talks about mandalas and endings. It says human beings are, in some sense, defined by endings. What do you think of that idea? Do you agree? Does the idea make you uncomfortable? Does it seem true?

2   Matt shares in chapter 10 about the large number of people who came forward claiming to be the "real Steph," thinking they were the ones who sent the sky lantern. Why do you think that is? What would you say to someone in that situation—reaching out for love and confirmation—even if you knew they weren't the true sender?

3   In chapter 11, Steph and Matt talk about a variety of

things, including thoughts about family, God, and death. Steph says there is no life after death, that it's just like falling asleep. Matt says if there is a God, then He is like a good father: loving, proud, and wanting good things for His children. What would you say to the two of them? Would you agree or disagree?

4 Have you ever been on your way to purposely meet a stranger? What was that like? How did you feel? How did you prepare?

5 In chapter 13, Steph talks about having a list of goals for the year, to make her life better. Have you ever made a list like that? If so, what was on it? If not, what sort of thing would you put on it?

CHAPTERS 14–18

1 In chapter 14, we hear the story of Steph's first child. These sorts of family decisions are difficult and often painful. How did you feel when you got to the end of the chapter? Do you think Steph's dad was proud of her for the choice she made?

2 Do you think the place you live in affects your thoughts and beliefs about yourself? How would your life be the same, better, worse, or different if you had grown up in a town like Tooele (or, if you did grow up in a place like Tooele, somewhere completely different—say, San Francisco or New York City)?

3 Matt realizes in chapter 16 that becoming friends with Steph proves there are amazing untapped connections that could be had with any number of people around him, including the strangers waiting to board a plane next to him. What do you think of his idea of connection? Do you think that the vast majority of strangers are just friends you haven't met yet? Are there people near you who are unlikely to be your friends? Either way, how do you know? How does this affect your relationship to those strangers? Do you think the way you are living is open or closed to those connections?

4 What do you think about the "level up" theory of parenting that Matt refers to in chapter 17? Do you think a new parenting challenge comes only after you've mastered the previous challenge? Does this seem naïve? Insightful? Silly? What would you say to a nervous young couple about to have their first child?

5 Chapter 18 suggests that, instead of teaching children to enjoy the things we love, we should learn what children love and find a way to bring our interests and theirs together, making something new. What do you think of this? Is this something your parents did? Is it something you do with children you love in your life?

CHAPTERS 19-22

1 Matt refers to Steph's father keeping her note to him for so many years as a sort of "emotional archaeology." What do you think of that term? What's your favorite way to be an emotional archaeologist (pictures, letters, movies, favorite smells or foods, etc.)?

2 Love is described as "a story" as well as "a dance" and "a hummingbird." What do you think about those metaphors? Do they work? Would you add to or subtract from them? If you had to say "Love is . . . ," what word would you use to finish the sentence? Why? How do your answers vary in your group?

3 There are several pieces of the three letters to Matt's

daughters that are identical to one another. Why do you think that is? Which parts of those letters would be true of your feelings and hopes for someone you love?

4   Is there someone who needs a letter from you? This could be a parent or friend, a child, or some other important person in your life. If you are comfortable sharing, tell your book club who it is and when you're going to write the letter. (There is a "How to Write a Letter to Your Child" resource included in this book.)

5   If Matt hadn't written his letter to Steph, he probably would not have ended up writing the letters to his daughters. It seems that doing a small kindness for a stranger ended up bringing good things back to Matt's family. What do you think of that idea? Is that what you would expect of the way the world works, or was it an unexpected fluke?

CHAPTERS 23-25

1   In chapter 23, Matt talks about his experiment in thinking of others and doing small acts of kindness through-

out the week. What would that look like in your life? Would you be willing to try to do an hour a week of kindnesses for others? If so, what do you think the result would be? Is there a charity or organization your group could volunteer an hour to serve together? Brainstorm some ideas and make a plan.

2   Matt also shares his own failure in staying focused on others when he talks about the young man in the car accident in chapter 23. He says the young man was "invisible" to him because he was focused on himself and his own needs. Are there "invisible" people in your own life? Who are they? How can you become more aware of their presence and their needs?

3   Chapter 24 describes a feeling of holiness when Matt and his friends and family launch their own sky lanterns. Have you ever experienced a feeling like that? When? Is it something you enjoyed? Do you want to experience it again?

4   Chapter 25 says "Friends are the miracle." Do you agree or disagree? Who are your best friends? What is it about them that made you so close?

5   What do you think about the last sentence in the book? What does it mean? Do you agree? How did you feel when you read it?

6   Now that you've reached the end of the book, what are your overall thoughts and feelings? Are there things about the book you want to share with other people? Who? If you could say one thing to the author, what would it be?

Ask the Author

What's your relationship with Steph like now?

Steph and I are great friends. We usually text a few times a week. We're working on getting our families together so they can all meet.

What was one of the most meaningful stories readers shared with you after reading your blog post?

One of the more moving stories came from a young woman whose husband had just passed a few months before. They had two small kids, and though he loved them desperately, his death was sudden and he never had the chance to leave behind any letters or videos for them. She printed a copy of my letter out and set it aside to give to the kids when they were older. She said it was exactly what he would have said to them if he had known he was leaving.

Maybe the most meaningful thing for me was watching how caring and kind people were as they passed the letter around. There was beauty in how people would read it and say, "My friend needs to hear these words," and then pass it along. The original letter went viral in large part due to the love and compassion of those who wanted to share it with others.

Why do you think your letter to Steph resonated with so many people?
I think for a moment people were reminded that love is real, it's a part of this world, it's powerful, and they deserve to have it in their lives. I wish every parent could share that message with his or her kids. Some do, some don't, some do it once, others do it often. But we all want that message. We all want to be reminded that there is love in the world, and our parent loves us. Love is stronger than we think, even on the bad days.

Have your kids read the letters you wrote them? What was their response?

I had planned to do this whole ritual where I took them out one by one and we would go to dinner and I would hand it to them, and then we would talk about it and I could tell them how much I loved them. What actually happened is that I was on a long plane ride with Zoey and Allie and they asked to read the manuscript and I said sure. A couple of hours later we were sitting in the air over the Pacific and they were both crying and hugging me and saying it was a good book. They loved the letters, and I am so thankful this book gave me the impetus to write them. I haven't read Myca's to her yet, but it's not that simple to get her in one place for five minutes.

You don't talk a lot about your own dad in this book. What's your relationship like?

My dad is great. He has always been—and continues to be—a loving, kind, generous person. He spends a lot of time with my kids. He's a private person, so I didn't think he'd enjoy me including a lot of stories about him in this book, but suffice it to say I'm deeply thankful for him and my mom, and many of my best insights about love and being loved come from growing up in their home. Thanks, Mom and Dad! Love you!

You mention the letter was translated into several languages. Where was the most astounding place a reader reached out to you from?

You could almost tell where the letter was spreading by the e-mails that arrived in my in-box each day. I knew almost to the moment when the letter hit the UK, and it spread within three hours to New Zealand and Australia. I was pretty amazed to get some notes from China and countries in eastern Europe. Basically, I feel like if I went on a world tour, I could visit with sky lantern people and always have a place to stay. Wouldn't that be cool?

Is there any update on your friend with cancer?

Shasta is, as of this writing, doing really well and on a stable treatment plan. We're all hopeful that, through medical advances or miraculous healing, she can be well for many years to come. If you'd like updates on this dear friend of ours, there is a Facebook group for her at https://www.facebook.com/shastakramerupdates.

Are you a spiritual person? There are some references to praying in this book, but you don't say much about God or religion.

Oh, yes, spiritual things are deeply important to me and a daily part of my life (and my family's). This book is about love for one another despite our differences. I didn't want to exclude any readers from the story by insisting that they listen to my own spiritual beliefs. A core part of what I believe, though, is that we have a debt of love to other human beings: it's an obligation and an honor to love one another. That can be hard work, but it also brings joy in our lives and can be part of the reparation of the world by demolishing unjust systems, healing the brokenhearted, and increasing the capacity of humanity to give and receive love. If you would like to know more about the particulars of my own faith journey, I am glad to share about that elsewhere, or you can check out some of my previously published books.

Any advice for parents?

Don't miss a chance to tell your kids you love them. Even if they don't respond, I promise they still want to hear it. Don't wait, don't chicken out, don't rationalize why you're not going to do it or say, "They already know." Say it often, say it honestly, say it without hesitation. If you're not sure how to do that, ask someone to help you.

Any last thoughts for your readers?

First, thank you! Thank you for reading this book and for encouraging others to do the same. Second, remember that the world is full of wonder and beauty and the potential to connect with the people around us. We can miss it so easily. Remember, I thought the sky lantern was trash, but it was a miracle. We may misidentify miracles as trash every day if we're not careful. Lastly I'd say, like any good dad: love others, be loved, and live a good life.

How to Write a Letter to Your Children

IT WAS A PRICELESS GIFT THAT DISCOVERING THE SKY LAN-
tern eventually led to me writing my daughters letters about
what they mean to me. If there is a child you love—a son or
daughter, a grandchild, a niece or nephew, or merely one
who is like family to you—you might like to write a letter,
too. Writing such a letter was hard but rewarding (for them
and for me!). Here are some tips, exercises, and ideas to get
you started:

1   **Short is good.** You could write a thirty-page letter, but you don't have to. You can write a great letter that's just a few paragraphs or even a few sentences. It's the quality of the words that matters, not the number.

2   **Accentuate the positive.** This letter is not the place to share things you wish your child was better at. "I love you even though you don't excel at football" is not a particularly happy sentence. Anytime you are tempted to say something like "I love you, but . . . ," drop that last word. This is not the time for it. This should be a letter a child can go to anytime they have doubts or have forgotten you love them and need the reminder. When you've finished your letter, go back through and remove any negative comments that may have crept in without you realizing it. No criticism, no complaints, no negative comparisons, no backhanded compliments. This letter celebrates the positive and intends to lift the child up.

3   **Be honest. Be vulnerable.** There are times when we're uncertain how our kids feel about us. It's hard not to withdraw or protect oneself when that happens. In this letter, just be honest. Don't shy away from being strong in expressing your deep love for them. Don't worry

about how they will react . . . and know that even if they don't respond the way you hope, your words are powerful, necessary, and transformative.

4 **Actually use the words *I love you* and *I am proud of you*.** In my experience, these are the two phrases children long to hear from their parents the most. Plus, that's two sentences that are already written for you! Make sure they know you love them because of who they are and not because of anything they've accomplished. This way they know that no matter what happens, you'll always love them.

Exercises that might help WHEN YOU SIT DOWN TO WRITE:

1 **Use photographs to jog your memory.** Go through old photographs of your child. What were some of your favorite times together? Why? What was it like in the hard times? How did your child change your life?

2 **Find a central metaphor for your letter.** You probably noticed my letters each had a central metaphor

(i.e., story, dance, and the hummingbird). I found those by asking some of these questions about my kids: What are your child's favorite things? Toys? Activities? Colors? People? What does this say about them? What does this say about their passions and interests? What things about those interests reveal something beautiful about your child? Finding a central theme helps in crafting the letter and making it unique to how you feel about your child.

3   **What do you wish you had heard from your parents?** If they wrote you a letter, what things did they say that were particularly meaningful to you, that you treasure? Write those things down. Is there something in what they said or you wish they had said that you would want to pass on to your own child?

I hope your child treasures your letter. Set aside some time right now and go write it!

How to Host Your Own
Sky Lantern Party

MOST OF US WHO CAME TOGETHER FOR OUR LITTLE SKY lantern party in the last two chapters of this book were truly moved by the experience. It was a beautiful, memorable bonding moment for us. If you want to host a sky lantern launch of your own, here are some tips on how to do that!

1 **Check into the local regulations related to sky lanterns.** Because an open flame is involved, it is illegal in some places (or during certain seasons) to launch sky lanterns. You may need a permit or a fire official present. Don't do anything illegal! You could be fined, or there could be damage to people or property.

2 **Find a suitable location.** You need to be at least five miles away from airports, and not directly near any major roads. While you might be tempted to do it in a crowded neighborhood, it's not a good idea. Make sure the lanterns will have plenty of room to rise. A large field is best: no trees, houses, or buildings nearby.

3 **Buy the highest quality lanterns you can find.** I bought biodegradable white lanterns from www.sky lanterns.us. You can get all different shapes and colors. Cheaper lanterns are more likely to tear (in which case they don't fly well) or burn (in which case they are on fire). Two of our ten lanterns didn't work, one because the fuel cell wasn't hot enough, and one because I stepped on it and tore the paper. (Whoops!) Higher-quality lanterns are less likely to have problems . . . and getting biodegradable lanterns is a great thing, as the

metal rings of non-biodegradable lanterns can harm wildlife.

4 **Bring permanent markers for decoration!** We let everyone write on our lanterns. Some people chose to do their own, and we had a few that were for everyone. Some people wrote wishes, prayers, favorite sayings, scriptures. Others drew patterns, funny pictures, or notes of thankfulness. (Make sure people know to be careful not to tear the paper.) We even had toddlers drawing on the lanterns. It was really fun.

5 **Make sure to have water and/or a fire extinguisher on hand.** Because the better lanterns are specially treated, they don't catch on fire easily. But things around the lantern can. It's wise to be prepared. Likewise, use lighters that are safe and easy to use, and that children won't wander off with.

6 **Don't fly lanterns under windy conditions.** Wind not only makes the lanterns fly unpredictably, it can also cause the fuel cell to knock into the lantern and burn a hole in it. It could crash to the ground and catch something else on fire.

7   **When you light the lantern, be patient before you release it.** It takes a little while for enough hot air to get into the lantern to cause it to rise. If you release it too early, it may skim along the ground. You should feel a light tug from the lantern when it's ready to be released.

8   **Make sure only adults light the lanterns.** And make sure children know not to run beneath the lanterns. They're beautiful and kids want to get near them. Remember, this is open flame. Use caution.

9   **Wait for dusk to launch the lanterns.** On launch day, I looked up the official sunset time on the Internet, and we met about an hour before that to decorate and hang out. We probably waited until about thirty minutes after official sunset to launch the lanterns. You can fly them any time of day, of course, but they're most beautiful in the dark.

10   **If a lantern doesn't fly, offer to let someone keep it.** It's really disappointing if you've decorated a lantern and it doesn't work for some reason. Offer to let the person who did the most work keep it, or take it home and cut

out the decorations and frame them for that person to remember the special experience.

11 **Bring your cameras.** We had such a great time, and we were all so happy that we took a lot of pictures and videos. Don't forget: a lot of the pictures will be taken in the dark! I don't know when or if we'll do it again, but it was a beautiful bonding time for all of us involved. We're thankful to have the memories and the pictures.

Contact Matt

Matt would love to hear from you! You can email him directly at SkyLantern@Mikalatos.com.

You can also follow Matt on Twitter (@mattmikalatos) or Facebook (facebook.com/mikalatosbooks).

Find more information about Matt, his books and more at Mikalatos.com.

If you would like to book Matt to speak at an event, please contact Ambassador Speakers at (615) 370-4700 or info@ambassadorspeakers.com.